VISITING THICH NHAT HANH:

AN AMERICAN IN PLUM VILLAGE

by

Starr Regan DiCiurcio

Anathapindika Press

Schenectady, New York 12309

For Thay

INTRODUCTION

There may come a time in your life when it is necessary to step out of all that is familiar in order to be known to yourself. If this is not done, it is probable that your life will pass as a series of routines performed — tranquilizing, numbing and ultimately deadening. Such a time came to me.

For many years I had privately been a dutiful child, wife and mother, and publicly a highly responsible professional with a series of successful performances. After being a public high school teacher for over a decade in a small, declining community in upstate New York, I was granted a semester-long sabbatical. My break enabled me to study Asian cultures, but before my work began I gave myself the gift of a month to study my lost self. I knew this study had to be done away from the comfort of my routines. Relationships and titles defined me. Life was full, too full. I was a content person who increasingly felt a sense of gliding along on the surface of my days. A longing arose in me for a deeper connection with life.

When asking myself what I wanted in my remaining years, I found myself lost, a stranger to my soul. Raised a Catholic by Irish-American parents, one Baptist and the other Catholic, I had turned to Buddhism several years before as an avenue to a fuller spiritual awareness. It was in meditation that I had glimpses of the lost woman within. Now on sabbatical she would be pursued.

Where better to do this than Plum Village? Through his writings Thich Nhat Hanh was the one who had brought me the Buddhist teachings that had begun to transform my life, like thousands of other Westerners. A prolific author, he has published over one hundred books that have been translated into twenty-two languages. I wanted to see his home away from home in France. His native land of Vietnam has been lost to him for over 30 years now. Nhat Hanh (Thich is a Vietnamese title for a monk) became a novice in the early 1940's at the age of sixteen. He was ordained a monk in 1949 and in the ensuing years he dedicated himself to the reform of Buddhism and to the peace movement. He became familiar with the West by studying and teaching at Princeton and Columbia and through his international peace work. Also through these efforts, he befriended Thomas Merton and Martin Luther King, Jr. who nominated him for the Nobel Peace Prize. Thich Nhat Hanh's work with the Buddhist Peace Delegation took him to Paris and eventually he made his home in France, at first just outside Paris and then in the south of the country where the monastic community of Plum Village was established.

In Plum Village's Winter Retreat I hoped to join him and the community in practice and to learn more about the teachings of the Buddha.

Ironically, learning about concepts such as emptiness and non-self taught me more about myself — my ego, and my attachments. It also taught me to laugh about it all, the great gift of joy. And at times meditation brought a true sense of freedom, which now seems to me to be the greatest gift of spiritual practice.

When I came home many friends, students and loved ones asked me about this trip. It was absurd to render a travelogue description of this experience, and I often ended up regretfully saying little or nothing. When genuine interest persisted, I shared the hen's scratches of the journal I had kept during my retreat. Encouraged again and again to write this little book, I offer it now to all those who are seekers, and especially to my children, Shanti and Chandan. May they be blessed always. I also offer it with love to the Vietnamese students I taught as they arrived in this country. They taught me so much more than I could ever hope to teach them — especially my cherished Goddaughter, Phuong.

My thanks go to my dear friend, Sharon Therriault, not just for wading through this manuscript, but more for her unfailing support and great caring spirit. And thanks to my cousin Nancy Forgette, talented photographer, for shivering out in Yaddo's gardens to get the jacket photo. Her friendship is a special gift to my life. To my husband, Tom, my eternal gratitude for all he has so generously given of himself to me for over a quarter of a century. There are no words to adequately describe his devotion to our family, and particularly to me in this endeavor. He is a prince among men.

And finally, this book is dedicated to Thich Nhat Hanh. Teacher among teachers, a bridge from the East to the West, it is he who opened Dharma doors for me.

The French countryside is bleak with a drizzling winter rain as my train moves leisurely from Paris to Bordeaux. The land is flat, and increasingly covered with the orderly rows of vineyards that produce the excellent wines of this region. I think of Thay's (Thich Nhat Hanh's title of teacher) teaching against alcohol and wonder at his choice of settling in the land famous for its production. As the train gets closer to my destination, Sainte Foy La Grande, hills come into view. Perhaps it is these hills that drew Thay. Certainly he loved the hills of his native Vietnam, and he might have been reminded of them here. They are gentle, graceful hills, which clearly could inspire this gentle, graceful monk I have come to visit.

The taxi driver speaks no English but has a warm smile and nods as I show him the address for Lower Hamlet, Plum Village. I rest in the back seat briefly, but then lean forward and strain to see all I can. I have never been comfortable speaking French but now I try to tell him that the view is "magnifique!" He turns, a bit startled that I have spoken and smiles. Then he begins to point out game birds and other delights as I smile back. Quickly I learn that the French are so much friendlier than their American reputation would suggest.

We approach a narrow lane and I see a sign for Plum Village. This is closely followed by another sign saying, "You Have Arrived." The wooden signs, one following another, remind me of the old Burma Shave ads that used to line the north country highways of my childhood. The words, so familiar through Thay's teachings, and the childhood remembrance, make me smile. At the end of the lane is a small group of gray stone buildings, clearly an old farm. It is overwhelmingly, romantically, beautiful to me. I don't know if this is because I have waited so long to see this special place, or if anyone would say the same. It is empty. This is immediately clear as we pull in. I pay the driver and he pulls away – as comfortable leaving me, as I am to be alone.

This is an unexpected gift. Time has been given to me here in Lower Hamlet to be by myself and, as if in understanding, the light rain has lifted and I begin to slowly walk around. This Hamlet is one of three. It, and Upper Hamlet, are the original settlement of Plum Village begun in 1982. Lower Hamlet currently houses the community's women. The original buildings face front and a small, oval drive takes me to all the additions. Old stone outbuildings have been made into housing units and a new construction looks a bit like an American motel. In the rear is a large meditation hall, called a zendo, and then I spot a small one in part of the main building. It is exquisite and instantly becomes my favorite spot in the monastery.

From my reading I know that the residents of the three Hamlets all gather in one place for Thay's Dharma talks on Thursdays and Sundays. Since it is Sunday, I am sure that is what is happening. So the emptiness does not worry me. My camera comes out and I take pictures of the buildings as I walk. With a feeling of reverence I intrude on no space, but simply walk around this small ring road a number of times, soaking up my surroundings. It settles my soul. The trip from New York has been long. I have been traveling for two days but now feel total comfort in this place. Leaving the road, I wander down to the pond and look at the brown, sleeping lotus plants. Their leaves are large and heavy and the pods are nodding in the late winter water. They are profuse even in their dormant state and you can sense their life ready to burst forth with the approaching spring. This reminds me of the Buddha's teaching on interdependence. What looks like a sodden, dead plant contains what will be the spectacular, blooming lotus. In the same manner, when the lotus is floating on the summer waters of this pond it will contain the decay and dormant state of what now is before me. So it is with all creation when we learn to look deeply. Ourselves included.

As the hill rises from the pond there are rows of plum trees standing in formal orchard formation. Closer to the buildings is a surprise — bamboo trees. There is one small grove with a bench in the center. My companions are several cats who undoubtedly have learned that Buddhists are good folks for animals to hang around. In the distance is a large, spectacular, white water bird, perhaps a type of crane. Signs of spring are here in small buds on plants, and flowers known at home as snowdrops. On close inspection, the bark of the trees is showing promising flecks of green.

My solitude is interrupted by the arrival of three nuns instantly recognizable by their plain brown robes and shaved heads. They are surprised to see me. Despite my phone calls, registration and letters, no one has remembered my arrival date. They have come to pick up a few forgotten things for lunch. It seems that will include me. Tucking my luggage in a small room, we are off.

The chatter in the car is light and warm as we travel the three kilometers to Upper Hamlet. They call me "sister", which touches me and gives a sense of belonging. We head into an old and majestic wooded area for walking meditation. We join a few others in single file on the well-worn path, and I feel self-conscious in my meditation. I have never really taken to walking meditation the times I have tried it. My mind seems to wander more than ever, and I feel clumsy walking slowly and deliberately. It feels like my whole body broadcasts this ineptitude to the serene monastics. All of a sudden they stop and move to the side. I look around trying to figure out what they are doing and then hear rustling sounds and quiet voices. Thay is coming. We have come upon the main group and they will need to pass us as Thay leads the walk's return. We all wait while Thay stops to speak to one of the nuns who had just driven me. I am drawn to watch everything and to lower my head at the same time. I end up doing some awkward combination; after all, the opportunity to observe Thay in close proximity is why I have come to the Winter Retreat. His summer retreats in the States attract close to a thousand participants, and here in the Winter Retreat at Plum Village, there are only a handful of guests. When he passes my head is lowered but I forget to bow. It is not necessary, but it is a sign of respect I wish to give. This is the man whose teaching has changed my life.

During the afternoon the sisters suggest resting in Transformation Hall, the meditation hall set aside for women that day. Near exhaustion, I try but find I cannot sleep on the floor of the hall. Some of the sisters are having a rollicking time rehearsing a skit. Even though they are speaking Vietnamese, what they are doing is clear. Others are scattered around the outside of the room, strategically trying to get the heat from radiators as they nap. I marvel at their ability to just relax and rest, and realize I probably have not taken a group nap since kindergarten. Across the room a lovely Black woman, who looks American, is doing yoga postures with mesmerizing grace and ease.

Hours pass. Many things go through my mind. Home floods back to me. My family, students, suburban American home, friends, — all seem so far away. The peacefulness felt in Lower Hamlet has deserted me and doubt sneaks in. Was this a mistake? Will I ever fit in here at all? I think of all I have learned from Thay's books and retreats and wonder at the strangeness I suddenly feel. I contemplate the Four Noble Truths. First, that life is full of suffering (as I am experiencing now), and second, that there are causes to that suffering. Third, comes the good news that we can stop our suffering through practice. And forth, the practice to end suffering consists of the Noble Eightfold Path: Right View, Right Thinking, Right Speech, Right Action, Right Livelihood, Right Diligence, Right Mindfulness and Right Concentration. But at this moment there is no comfort.

Finally, we are going to the cars to return to Lower Hamlet and tears are streaming down my face. A young nun checks on me and guides the way with a flashlight. I assure her, and myself, that I am fine, just feeling deep fatigue. She talks to me kindly about her vocation and how she came to this community from the States via her college world religions course. In the pitch black darkness she tells of her struggle with her family and her cross-cultural identity. Although we will be living in the Lower Hamlet community together for the next several weeks, this intimate sharing is the only conversation we have.

Monday, January 31

After twelve hours of sleep and a shower I am a new person. That terrible sense of complete vulnerability, that seems to strike me in the depths of fatigue, has left. Alone when I awoke, I took a good look around my charming room this morning. Certainly I have been lucky to be assigned to this old fieldstone building called Persimmon. On the first floor are the communal bath and some rooms hidden behind closed doors. Upstairs more rooms are tucked under the eaves, including mine. Each room is named for a bird and mine is called Peacock. Many of the women ushered into this room must seem like peacocks to the nuns. It is simple and lovely with four beds, four white chairs, and a tall set of wooden shelves. The beds are covered with cheery, red print comforters. The head of my bed is tucked in a corner against the outside wall, which has a charming oval window only about a foot long. Since it is set in the stone wall, there is a wide sill where I place my tiny bronze Buddha next to the small flower arrangement left by the woman who was here before me. A sweet gift of thoughtfulness. Above me two modern skylights contrast with these very old walls. All in all, I am sure the room is one of the nicest here, but maybe everyone feels that way about their space. My two roommates are kind and warm even though we have spoken very little; one is American and the other Belgium.

11

The dining room is located in part of the original farmhouse. It clearly is action central for the community's daily life, like the kitchen in many American homes. Benches flank long, wooden tables and a woodstove gives off welcome heat. On one wall is a large blackboard that contains notices for the Sangha (the community). The critical information of the day's schedule is there. Also, there is a sign posted for those retreatants who are regularly fasting at certain meals, and others have added their names to the blackboard for this particular day. I had not thought about making any eating discipline a part of this time, but I know it is a good idea for me. Skipping meals seems not to be the commitment I can make on the spur of the moment, so I quickly decide that I will make it my practice not to take seconds of anything for this time. This, I hope, will heighten my awareness of nourishing myself properly and at the same time be a manageable commitment.

Food is a big issue for Americans, including myself. We consume so much, and in a way that does so much damage to ourselves and others. Enormous numbers of Americans are suffering from obesity and related health issues. In order to support our fast food industry, we raise grain for cattle when that same grain could feed so many more people than those fed by the meat produced. We pollute our waters with the waste of the cattle and destroy valuable lands, including the rainforests, to create thousands of grazing acres for them.   Antibiotics and other drugs are introduced into the food system to get greater yields, and new health concerns are created.   It is a complicated and sad story that we do not want to look at because it affects our way of life, seems an inconvenience and sacrifice.   But on our conscience rests the 40,000 lives of children lost every day to hunger and diseases of malnutrition.   We must ask ourselves one question. What do we really need? The Buddhist practice of mindful consumption is powerful in the face of this challenge.   Here in Plum Village we only eat a vegetarian diet. Although a longtime vegetarian, it is a real bonus for me to do so in community.   As Thay teaches, we are fortunate to be able to eat in this way.

In the center of the dining room is a pillar where some mail is tacked up for all to enjoy.   In addition, there are a couple of lists, one of work groups, and one of tasks for them.   The first one makes me smile with its child-like, simple images of beauty for work group titles; the second makes me wonder what lies ahead.

Work Groups
White Clouds
Green Papaya
Warm Hearth
Flowing River
Moonlight
Winter Sunshine
Blue Skies
Sweet Potato

Job Rotation

Pot Washing
Bell
Cleaning
Available for Community Work
Cooking
Rest
Available for Community Work
Available for Community Work

A small altar is set up on one of the cupboards lining the side walls. Before the Buddha, fruit and flowers are arranged. Above, on the stone wall, is a sign I love: "The Bread in Your Hand is the Body of the Whole Cosmos." The vegetarian fare is laid out buffet style on one of the long tables, and when all is ready the large, outside bell calls the community to the meal. Before taking a plate each person pauses and briefly reflects. We sit and wait for all to be served, then the bell at the altar is rung and the Five Contemplations are recited.

1. This food is the gift of the whole universe – the earth, the sky and much hard work.
2. May we live in such a way as to be worthy to receive it.
3. May we transform our unskillful states of mind and learn to eat with moderation.
4. May we take only foods that nourish us and prevent illness.
5. We accept this food to realize the path of understanding and love.

All of us eat in silence for about twenty minutes and then we are able to talk quietly toward the end. Some people choose not to talk and others enjoy socializing. The main meal is at noon and the food is excellent. Coconut milk is succulent in the first Plum Village stir-fry I taste. The coleslaw is lush with tomatoes, apples, carrots, raisins and other delights.

The nuns and monks carry bowls that they fill carefully with heavy foods on the bottom and lighter ones on the top. The idea is that the bowl they have is sufficient. The idea of sufficiency is important and one I need to reflect on much more. Certainly Americans are so automatically driven to gathering all that we can – in food, money, possessions, even relationships, that it becomes problematic. Less is often more, and quality is as important a concept as quantity, but our culture drives us. There are signs that many people are increasingly aware of the burden this places on individual Americans, and the societal injustice it creates for the world. So I reflect on what is sufficient, not just on my plate but also in my life. This is a road to freedom.

In the afternoon we have a break and I read a transcript of one of Thay's Dharma talks, "Helping the Baby Buddha to be Born." Here he talks about the 84,000 Dharma doors. Although he notes that this expression is an exaggeration he explores the idea that these doors keep opening for future generations to know the Buddha's teachings. I love the dynamic nature of this concept – the idea that change is natural, desired and necessary. I also am drawn to the idea of the 84,000 doors of revelation. I know that Thay is one of those doors and, in fact, now he is the one for me. Even as a child I had trouble with the idea of "the one, true Church." How could that be? My parents were both Irish-American Christians but the divide between my mother's Protestant heritage and my father's Catholic heritage was tragic. Both families disapproved of their marriage. They were isolated for years, and a lot of suffering was created by this intolerance. Always close, my parents dealt with their difference in silence. My mother never attended any church but prayed with her Bible. With my father, she raised us strictly according to the teachings of the Roman Catholic Church. But her exclusion from the family's practice and prayer was confusing to me as a child. Kneeling by my bed at night I would finger my rosary meditatively saying the familiar prayers and contemplating the mysteries we were taught based on the life of Jesus. When footfalls approached, I would tuck the rosary in my hand and dive under the bed as if searching for something. Was it right to pray? Did it hurt my mother to see a rosary in my hand? Was I disloyal to her? Through some silent agreement, such questions were never asked. How could my mother have been expected to swallow all that discrimination without becoming angry and hurt? How could my mother's Baptist church be less worthy than my father's Catholic church then, or now? And why would a loving God reveal teachings to only one, small group? And further, beyond this ecumenical divisiveness, were the Christians of the world to believe that other faiths brought no enlightenment to humanity?

At the evening meal the tables with lay people are full so I sit with two nuns. Actually I am not sure if they are two nuns or a monk and nun. It can be difficult to tell, especially among the very young monastics, and although we are in the women's Hamlet visiting back and forth between Hamlets is accepted. Other lay practitioners begin a new table and three more nuns join mine. I feel increasingly uncomfortable and finally break the silence to ask if it is acceptable to be there. They laugh and welcome me warmly. It seems people simply sit where they like and there is a natural inclination to sit with those you know. I am aware of how hard I am concentrating on the routines, trying to understand the customs and rules through observation. It can be hard to decipher.

At evening meditation we gather in the small zendo that had so appealed to me yesterday. It is part of the original buildings so the walls are gray fieldstones and the serene, candle-lit Buddha is golden. The round blue meditation cushions (zafus) rest on large, flat, square cushions (zabutons); they are lined in neat rows on the hardwood floors and one has my name in front of it. The smells of incense and the wood-burning stove warm us in the damp night. We face the walls and sit for about a half hour. My mind is restless as I continue to take in my surroundings. At the sound of the bell we walk slowly in meditation around the hall. We sit again but facing center this time, and the nuns chant for Thay's sister who has just recently died. Although the words are in Vietnamese it is easy to sense their meaning and the chanting itself is mesmerizing. In the evening hours we observe Noble Silence, a practice of not speaking to encourage meditative experience. At 9:45 I am ready to sleep again. As all darkens around me I feel the great distance I have traveled. Images float through my mind as I drift off – sweet moments with loved ones, raucous ones with students, strains of music. So far away as to seem unreal, and then gone.

Tuesday, February 1

Each day I read the Gospel of my Roman Catholic heritage and reflect on it. It is my way of giving direction to my thoughts about my root faith during this retreat. Yesterday's reading was about Jesus removing the impure spirits from the poor, chained, isolated man and putting them into swine who then drowned. My only feeling about this was for the poor pigs! That's the Buddhist in me. Today's reading strikes home. It is the story of the woman who touches Jesus' cloak in order to be cured. The strength and simplicity of this demonstration of faith is palpable. How difficult this would be with the crowds all around! And then when Jesus wants to know who this is; the courage she must have needed to come forward. Here we have the imbalances — between man and woman, and between spiritual leader and follower — healed along with the illness. And the healing is made possible through mutual action, the faith of the woman and the loving-kindness of Jesus.

My sleep was fitful but I am up at 4:30 for 5:30 meditation. Downstairs in Persimmon I find a small room where I can do my morning yoga sun salutations. This will probably be my only yoga practice while here, but it is better than none. At this early hour the space is mine alone and I enjoy stretching out before I sit. The Abbess here, Sister Jina, is from Belgium and was a yoga teacher before joining the order. Perhaps she still does yoga postures, asanas, when she gets up. Yoga may be a spiritual practice in itself, but it also has the potential to be a support to any such pursuit. It assists in the integration of body, mind and spirit that so many people are seeking today. I find it relaxes the mind and body so the spirit may come forth. If one is enjoying a sitting practice, the yoga can help prepare the body physically for this seemingly inactive act. The actual positioning of the body and the maintenance of a correct posture are both greatly aided by the physical discipline of yoga. And yoga teaches one to relate to the breath in a conscious manner, which is complementary to mindfulness.

I hear Thay's car arrive and he sits with us for The Five Mindfulness Trainings. He is silent but his presence lends power and beauty to the gathering. There are not many of us, probably around twenty, so the atmosphere is intimate in the zendo. The rows are arranged by seniority in the practice, and by length of stay in Plum Village. The young girl sitting next to me gestures for me not to get up during recitation of the Three Refuges because she has not taken the Mindfulness Trainings and she assumes I have not, since I am seated below her. This was a mistake and I am a little distressed because I am sure this is wrong. But I hope this chance will come again in my stay and I'll be able to stand. I can feel this striving in myself, the result of a lifetime's training to achieve. There is a Buddhist teaching on aimlessness and it is a tough one –

to let go, not aspire, to simply be in the present. My ego repeatedly gets in my way, but my eyes are on it.

The Five Mindfulness Trainings are the heart of my Buddhist practice. They are vows that I took when on my first summer retreat with Thay. Quietly in my room one night I wrote my letter of aspiration. Then at the end of the retreat, along with many others, I listened and recited the Trainings. My heart, mind and spirit were immediately and totally at home with these practices. They touched me profoundly and that day I received my certificate from Sister Chan Khong. On it was the Dharma name that Thay had chosen for me and tears filled my eyes as I read it: Boundless Lamp of the Heart. The Mindfulness Trainings provide me with a constant challenge to grow in my humanity. In some traditions they are known as The Five Precepts. Thay's choice of the words "mindfulness trainings" reminds me that they are a daily practice for continual renewal. Although they are clear in restrictions, it is the positive nature of them that strongly appeals to me. So it is not enough to not steal, one must be generous. And it is not enough to not lie; one must listen deeply and speak thoughtfully. In discussions in the States, the most controversial admonition is against the taking of any alcohol. In the retreat Thay was adamant about this. His position is that alcohol has caused such havoc in our world that it must not be drunk, and valuable grain must not be used to produce it. Even if we think we can handle drinking as individuals, we have a responsibility to others not to drink, for any drinking contributes to the whole pattern of destruction. I have been struck with how difficult this restriction is for people to accept. This level of resistance alone has convinced me of the correctness of Thay's teaching.

After sitting, the ceremony begins with the lighting of incense and recitation of The Three Refuges, sometimes called The Three Jewels.

The Three Refuges

1. I take refuge in the Buddha,
   the one who shows me the way in this life.

2. I take refuge in the Dharma,
   the way of understanding and love.

3. I take refuge in the Sangha,
   the community that lives in harmony and awareness.

****

The first Refuge honors the Buddha. He is not worshipped as a God, but he is respected as an enlightened being who gave the world a path for a meaningful life that can overcome suffering. The second Refuge is in the Dharma, the body of teachings of the Buddha. And the third Refuge is the Sangha, the community of practice. It is these three aspects of Buddhism that comprise a practice, and enable it to survive in a pressured, secular world.

The morning darkness, the incense, and candlelight create a warm atmosphere as we continue with the recitation of The Five Mindfulness Trainings. All my concentration is on these words.

The Five Mindfulness Trainings

1. Aware of the suffering caused by the destruction of life, I am committed to cultivating compassion and learning ways to protect the lives of people, animals, plants, and minerals. I am determined not to kill, not to let others kill, and not to condone any act of killing in the world, in my thinking, and in my way of life.

2. Aware of the suffering caused by exploitation, social injustice, stealing and oppression, I am committed to cultivating loving kindness and learning ways to work for the well being of people, animals, plants, and minerals. I will practice generosity by sharing my time, energy, and material resources with those who are in real need. I am determined not to steal and not to possess anything that should belong to

others. I will respect the property of others, but I will prevent others from profiting from human suffering or the suffering of other species on Earth.

3. Aware of the suffering caused by sexual misconduct, I am committed to cultivating responsibility and learning ways to protect the safety and integrity of individuals, couples, families, and society. I am determined not to engage in sexual relations without love and a long-term commitment. To preserve the happiness of myself and others, I am determined to respect my commitments and the commitments of others. I will do everything in my power to protect children from sexual abuse and to prevent couples and families from being broken by sexual misconduct.

4. Aware of the suffering caused by unmindful speech and the inability to listen to others, I am committed to cultivating loving speech and deep listening in order to bring joy and happiness to others and relieve others of their suffering. Knowing that words can create happiness or suffering, I am determined to speak truthfully, with words that inspire self-confidence, joy and hope. I will not spread news that I do not know to be certain and will not criticize or condemn things of which I am not sure. I will refrain from uttering words that can cause division

or discord, or that can cause the family or the community to break. I am determined to make all efforts to reconcile and resolve all conflicts, however small.

5. Aware of the suffering caused by unmindful consumption, I am committed to cultivating good health, both physical and mental, for myself, my family, and my society by practicing mindful eating, drinking and consuming. I will ingest only items that preserve peace, well-being, and joy in my body, in my consciousness, and in the collective body and consciousness of my family and society. I am determined not to use alcohol or any other intoxicant or to ingest foods or other items that contain toxins, such as certain TV programs, magazines, books, films, and conversations. I am aware that to damage my body or my consciousness with these poisons is to betray my ancestors, my parents, my society, and future generations. I will work to transform violence, fear, anger, and confusion in myself and in society by practicing a diet for myself and for society. I understand that a proper diet is crucial for self-transformation and for the transformation of society.

It is easy to see that these trainings are not things to be accomplished. I have heard Thay explain that they are our North Star. They have given me particular goals and, in general, have placed my life on a fruitful path. At times I just choose a single aspect as a practice. Recently it has been deep listening. For me, this has been a revelation. I thought I was a fairly good listener until I practiced deep listening. Now I stop all else while listening, all thought, all activities, all distractions are held at bay. My whole self is present. As a teacher this produced a dramatic change in my classroom. It had seemed like efficiency to deal with a number of students at once as I took attendance, pulled out handouts, and opened to a reading. I could point to the assignment on the board while gently turning a student around in his seat and announcing an after school activity. This was the normal pace. What a change to stop everything and listen just to the student in front of me. When others began to interrupt I'd simply hold up my hand and, if necessary, stop and explain that this was so-and-so's turn, and yours will come. The really amazing parts were the students' tolerance, which I didn't expect, and the increased efficiency. Listening in mindfulness makes people feel cared for, promotes understanding and just generally makes all go more smoothly. These are examples of the fruits of the practice.

After meditation, the bell calls us to breakfast. I go into the dining room and am startled to see Thay seated in a white lawn chair at the end of one of our long tables. I am so taken aback I don't even bow. This I realize as I stand in line to get my food, mortified. Welcome back, my ego! I need to let go.

After breakfast another bell announces the morning gathering. Back in the dining room, minus Thay, we form a circle. I am introduced along with one other newcomer from Paris. There are some announcements and we rehearse a chant. Then we are all given our work assignments. I had seen mine listed on the board as cleaning the red candle. I thought this must be some important candle! It ended up being the name of the small zendo where we just had our morning meditation. I am so happy to be given this job. The zendo has its own cleaning supplies that are used only in that room. After one of the sisters gets me started, I dust the altar and side tables, sweep, vacuum the small central carpet, line up the zafus and zabutons, and water the plants. Going slowly, sister reminds me that this is not work, it is working meditation and meant to be done meditatively. This is something to practice. The urge to rush comes repeatedly so I pretend that whatever surface I am sweeping, smoothing, washing, mopping, etc., is the Buddha's body. This is an old practice I had read about and it really helps. After, there is the hall to mop and the bathroom to clean so it is a full morning's work, or to the more enlightened, a full morning's meditation.

Late morning the community bell rings for walking meditation. The skies have cleared and the resultant good cheer is palpable. But a truly special time comes toward the end of the walk. I am hand in hand with one of the young women who is in residence here for several months. When I first learned walking meditation it had been uncomfortable for me to walk holding hands with strangers. I still never initiate this, but now it is fine when one of the Sangha takes my hand. So I am in comfort. The countryside church's bells begin to peel over and over, sound layering sound. We both stop and listen. In the zendo we often say a gatha, or prayer, when the bell is rung. It begins, "I send my heart along with the sound of the bell..." The sending of my heart along with these bells is breathtaking. The ringing seems to transport me into the universe. The others walk on, but without a word between us, we stay. As the bells end we walk back to the front of the Hamlet, bow to each other and go our separate ways.

Today we have a Dharma discussion group scheduled for the afternoon. This is especially for the small group of laywomen who are living at Lower Hamlet. So we meet in the Red Candle Zendo and gather on our cushions in a circle. What a small, yet diverse, group we are! There are women from France, Switzerland, Brazil, Spain, Sweden, the States, and Asian countries. Although only a few of us speak English as our native language, it is the language of choice of the group. Just one person needs an interpreter and one of the participants fills the role. I am impressed with this little demonstration of the growing universality of English.

We begin with a brief centering led by one of the long-term residents. Centerings are a way to come into the present moment, usually done by focusing on the breath in some manner. This may be a simple counting of the breath, or repeating words or phrases with each inhale and exhale. After settling in, we are asked to share something that gave us joy today, which certainly is not hard for any of us to do. Several mention the spectacular early morning sunrise; to me it was as if Van Gogh's most vibrant palette had been streaked across the night. I talk about waking up during the night, still a victim of lingering jetlag, and propping myself up on my elbows to look out the small window over my bed. My gift is to see the sparkling display of stars. The rainy skies had cleared and it looked as though I could reach out and touch these beacons of heaven. The discussion goes on to the concepts of emptiness and non-self and what they mean to us. These are not easy to grasp or articulate but the discussion is interesting and it allows us to get further impressions of each other. When silence is kept most of the time, it is difficult to get to know others, or to be known. One of the women shares that she is unhappy she came here during the Tet preparations. It is busy but, since I have no other experience in Plum Village, I have no basis for comparison. Some people offer supportive sympathy, and others urge her to be open to the experience just as it is offered to her.

Later, I speak to her alone and share with her how I failed to meet my own needs when I arrived.

It would have been so much wiser to have told the sisters who found me in Lower Hamlet on my first day, that I was tired and needed to rest. But my need to not bother anyone was greater, and that was foolish. My concern with their perceptions of me was really another surfacing of my ego. In the end taking care of our needs, as best we can, assists the community.

Wednesday, February 2

Today at our morning gathering we learn a song and then there are some announcements. One of the nuns asks permission to go to a doctor's appointment. The details of when, why, transportation, and so forth are arranged. Then our abbess talks to us in what seems to be a reference to the Dharma discussion of yesterday. She talks about the practice. She says that even when we are busy we can practice stopping, and that this is something we can continue when we go home. This is the monumental challenge, isn't it! Can one take a practice and bring it into daily life? Can the mindfulness found on the cushion be brought into the daily activities of the monastery, and then into the daily activities of our lives?

The preparations for Tet are underway. This celebration of the New Year is the most widely celebrated holiday of the Vietnamese people. The nuns are very busy and the air can be festive or tense, and at times both. It reminds me of the days before Christmas when there is such joy and pressure. This morning we are going to Upper Hamlet to make moon cakes and earth cakes. They are made of the same ingredients but the round ones are called moon cakes, and the ones that are rectangular, or square, are called earth cakes. I am able to catch a ride with some of the sisters so I arrive early. Thay is in the dining hall talking to some of the men on retreat here. At one end of the room all the waiting ingredients are carefully arranged in giant pots and pans. The banana leaves are so clean they gleam and one of the sisters is kneeling and using her hands to mix some green dye into the vat of rice. Thay comes by to look over the food. He converses in Vietnamese and seems to be giving instructions on the hanging of the New Year's banners. He seems so relaxed and quietly happy. After a short while he leaves, and everyone from Lower Hamlet and New Hamlet arrives. We sit at the long tables making the cakes, and chatting away in a festive spirit. Our little assembly lines all seem to have experts and novices and there are lots of jokes about the right way to tie the cakes. People move from table to table and we get to know a lot more about each other in this unusual holiday atmosphere. A young American, who is interested in a teaching career in English for Speakers of Other Languages, wants to talk to me. Then I meet an older nun from a Tibetan order who is considering a change to this community. Also here is a European woman whose young husband is dying and an American whose son was shot on a city street there. It is amazing how quickly we tell our stories and everyone knows our suffering and joy. Through it all, the festivity of the occasion permeates the room. At one point I look up and Thay is back taking string to some of the tables. He seems like a kindly uncle at a family reunion. This must be a particularly treasured time for him.

I head back to Lower Hamlet early because today I am assigned to dinner preparation. At lunch yesterday we ate in our work groups, or families; mine is called White Clouds. There are about six of us, and we rotate with the other groups to do routine chores utilizing working meditation, such as pot washing, cleaning, cooking, and community work. The "available for community work" days, are days we do special assignments such as cleaning cars or lanterns.

Before preparing dinner, my White Clouds family gets organized by discussing the menu and dividing up the tasks. One of the long-term residents is in charge since she loves to cook and the nuns in our group are busy with other things. We light the kitchen incense and begin to work in silence. Food is not consumed during preparation and nothing is wasted. All is done with meticulous attention to detail. The meal is light. I work on the soup and salad which ends up a feast of apples, endive, red peppers, black olives, cucumbers and lemon juice.

My meditation experiences continue to fluctuate. Last night's sitting was challenging for me. It was totally silent for an hour and a half with a short walking meditation once around the hall midway through. My back had a pain across it that forced me to self-consciously change my legs' position before the end. It was the first time that has ever happened to me. Perhaps it is from a sudden increase in sitting time, or maybe it is all that mopping, sweeping, etc., yesterday. My body certainly isn't used to that! If this continues, I may have to take a chair instead of a cushion, but my pride rears up at the thought of that. Hello, my American competitive streak! Am I sitting to create an ideal image of myself? Is it possible for me to sit for the divine good, and not for me?

Luckily this morning's sitting goes better. It is beautiful to walk in the darkness to the zendo, feeling the soft, cool rain on my face. I keep bundled from neck to ankles, in my long, tweedy, wool coat enjoying this closer contact with the weather. This coat, one of my mother's last gifts to me, is like a hug from her. Back home I just drive, literally and figuratively, through the elements. How much is missed! My heart remembers me as a little girl who spent so much time outdoors learning to love nature in all its rich variety. Where is that little girl?

When I settle on my cushion I hear intermittent, animal-like sounds coming from the next room. My mind keeps going to chickens, birds and the cats I've been making friends with here. Perhaps this sentient being is trapped in some way. Is this a moral dilemma – to sit or to rescue? Why can't I identify it? My thoughts are flying like monkeys through the treetops. I sit.

Tonight's sitting is optional so I have decided not to go since I still have to mop the hall floors in

Persimmon. The day is almost over and it has been fun, but long. There is so much to take in and I don't want to miss anything. I keep trying to be present in the moment and as long as I have practiced this teaching, it is always an imperfect practice, and I think it always will be. Living in community is challenging for me. I am accustomed to a highly private and independent lifestyle. In the days ahead I'll have reason to reflect on this.

Today's Gospel reading is the Presentation in the Temple. Simeon was long familiar to me but today I found Anna, a prophetess who had been living in a temple fasting and praying for as many years as I have been alive. Granted Gospel exaggeration, she was undoubtedly a woman of exceptional faith and vision. Why is it that Simeon is the one known to me? Undoubtedly he is the one taught more, but I have read this passage myself many, many times and Anna seems totally new to me. I think this must be my own acculturation to see the hero before seeing a heroine. How much have I missed? How often have I failed to enrich myself, or to celebrate my fellow women? Well, Anna will stay with me now.

Today's Gospel reading is the Mission of the Twelve. As Jesus sent his disciples off two by two, so Thay is doing now. Each month his monks and nuns go to Paris twice. They go in pairs and they go once to practice with the Sangha there in Vietnamese, and once in French. There is a delicate balance held between offering the teachings of Buddha to all and not proselytizing. Although from the make-up of the community itself it is clear that many leave other religions to join Thay, that conversion is not something he seeks. He teaches the value of keeping the spiritual practice of your heritage and enriching it with Buddhist thought. This he compares to a tree made stronger by the support of two roots instead of one. It is an image that is very meaningful for me as I grow in my Buddhist practice and participate in my Christian church as well.

The growth and vitality of this community is immediately evident. It has mushroomed to over 100 monks and nuns, most of them quite young. One nun here is only thirteen. They come from all over the world and this adds a beauty and strength that radiates through the monastery. It also makes the organization more complex to administer. The effects of this can be seen in small ways rather regularly. I was not expected on my arrival; one of my roommates arrived with a friend, called three times to be picked up at the train and never was. Visitors can feel isolated and neglected. One friend left early in disappointment. Another was told on the phone she could not bring her family, and on arrival that was changed. Of course they were not with her, but they joined her. Work can be problematic as retreatants adjust to their hamlets. Beyond the regular work schedule, monastics may ask for assistance that one can decline to give, but that seems to be the theory and not the practice. Who can say no to one of these saintly beings? Lazy day is cherished each Monday. There is little routine and the aim is to rest. This promised time can be lost if help is needed. The daily schedule is on the dining room board each morning but it is certainly subject to change. Here you really need to be able to let go of expectations. Fitting into community life means letting go of the ego a bit more, being flexible and keeping your sense of humor!

Last Sunday I missed the Dharma talk as I traveled to Plum Village. I have asked several of my fellow retreatants about the talk but they are pretty tongue tied about explaining it. This is a feeling that I often get when people ask me about Thay. It is like trying to get your tongue around the moon or the sun. Impossible! One powerful teaching was shared from that morning: when we cease being grateful, we begin to suffer. I think I should put that in a place where I see it each day. So much wisdom is held in those few words.

Thursdays are also Dharma talk days and today we go to New Hamlet for Thay's teaching and lunch. The New Hamlet is, of course, the newest of the three. While you can walk between Lower and Upper Hamlets, it is necessary to drive to New Hamlet. There seem to be more French speaking people here and it is predominantly, but not exclusively, female in composition. There are a number of couples and the atmosphere seems very relaxed to me. The buildings are again a mixture of old and new. In addition to these three hamlets for year-round residents, there are two more sites that are used in the months when large retreats are held at Plum Village.

The Dharma talk is organized into two parts. The first is a reading of paragraphs from the <u>Sutra on the Pure Land</u> and commentary by Thay. This is the Sutra now under study by the community. Pages rustle as Thay teaches and I follow along as best I can, but I have no written copy. It is fascinating to hear Thay use English, French, Vietnamese and Chinese – such impressive linguistic skill! At certain points he says that scholars need to look at this particular translation because it is in error. The Dharma is seen as a living, changing truth so different from our Western idea of an absolute truth, thought to be fixed and revealed.

Thay talks about our ten channels. He draws a pie on the board and divides it up into man, animal, self-enlightened being, Buddha, gods, hungry ghosts, bodhisattvas, Asura, etc. Asura, he explains, is a type of god that lives in good material conditions but is full of anger. I know a lot of Asuras. The idea of channels is interesting. When one of these channels is manifested in us, the others are still there. Each of us is like a television set that is turned to one station. If that particular station is bad, we don't throw the set out, we change the channel. Each of our cells has all channels. Our transformation must take place at our base, not on the surface. This is also beautifully illustrated by saying that each seed contains all seeds. This leads Thay to reflect on the dangers of genetic manipulation and the need to offer wisdom for the future of science and of us all.

After a tea break, we have the second part of the Dharma talk. This is about the five obstacles that interfere with our progress to the Pure Land. So what is it exactly that gets in our way to heaven, or enlightenment? The first obstacle really strikes home for me. It is time. Thay talks to us about the Western concept of time and the way we create time pressure. This causes a loss of freedom as we give up our opportunity to be truly alive. When we equate time with money, we are no longer free; we have created an obstacle to life. Time runs out before we have enough for ourselves and those we love. There is no time to sit, no time to breathe.

Thay instructs us to restore the kind of time that allows us to be truly alive. He suggests that we do what we aspire to, not just chase after things like fame and money. He recalls how our ancestors did not have all our modern conveniences but they had more time. Time is life. Find more time to be with nature and family.

Thay shares several examples of the use of time in Vietnam. At birthday celebrations you can arrive at any time of day, and you may stay for several days. Families send out invitations to have friends and loved ones come and celebrate the blooming of a cherry tree. If the tree doesn't choose to bloom on schedule, drums are beaten at the base of the tree to encourage it. He speaks of simple people taking a sampan out into the water and putting tea into a floating lotus flower. The flower closes up around the tea and is left overnight. Early the next morning they return to the flower and place it in a teapot to prepare a wonderful, fragrant tea party. I wonder what Thay will find when he returns to Vietnam. I hope some of these enchanting memories will still be waiting for him.

I remember my mother lamenting the invention of the car and how it changed visiting between families. Before that time she remembered taking a carriage to visit, and the visits would often be for several days. She and Thay would have enjoyed talking about the pitfalls of "progress." My own life is filled with time pressures. I often feel that nothing lasts for longer than a ten- or fifteen-minute segment of time; and the segments follow one another in a crushing, never-ending flow. This is the rhythm of the culture I live in, but at least it can be seen with an objective eye. It is the result of the required busy-ness for membership in today's American middle class. Some are breaking out of the pattern but they are few. Some new to the society never accept it. How refreshing it is for me to visit some of my students' homes. They are immigrants who are neighbors now, usually financially poor but able to drop everything when a guest arrives, sit over a cup of tea, and share their ordered, unhurried, and abundant lives. For the rest of us it is hard to resist all that we have been taught establishes our self worth – the accumulation of possessions, titles, power and money. But this vision ensnares our very lives. No wonder we now see such an increased craving for spiritual experience.

The second obstacle in our spiritual journey is the pollution of views. Here too, there is much food for thought. Thay has broken this challenge into five parts. First is the view that this body is who I am and I am limited to it. Second is the view of extremes, and the resultant need to follow the Middle Way. Third are wrong views. Forth is attachment to our views. This occurs when we are sure we hold the truth and we are no longer open to ideas. This narrowness diminishes our freedom. And last is an attachment to rules and rituals.

The third obstacle to spiritual progress is afflictions, such as anger, craving, confusion, etc. The forth obstacle is other living beings who do not support spiritual practice. The last obstacle is the concept of lifetime. Thay warns us about the danger of going in cycles. It is not correct to see our lives as birth, death, birth, death, going nowhere and it is not right to live in destructive cycles of marriage, divorce, marriage, divorce, or job after job. Once again he has taken these ancient teachings and made them a part of our day-to-day lives.

At walking meditation today Thay is followed by a young monastic whose assignment is to assist him as needed. This fortunate task seems to rotate daily among the monks and nuns. Following them is a young couple, and then myself and a fellow American retreatant. About a hundred people are behind us, the current population of the three hamlets. Formal lunch follows. Thankfully at Plum Village formal lunch does not entail the nightmare of oryoki, the nesting sets of Japanese Zen bowls. The few times I have tried to manage those, they have tripped me up. Probably that means I should embrace them as lessons in humility and patience, but these days I am glad not to have that extra instruction. Here we line up according to seniority in the community and then we take our food to the meditation hall and sit in rows, eating in silence. The women are on one side of the hall and the men on the other but a few people always seem to stray from that pattern. As far as I can see, no one corrects them. One learns mainly in time, through observation of the community's practice. We sit facing one another and chew mindfully as Thay has taught. Several elder nuns are visiting from Vietnam and they sit across from Thay. They also have attendants watching over them. The atmosphere is quiet and relaxed.

When eating is finished Thay rings the large bell at his side. In walks a beautiful young nun in her formal yellow robe. A sister gives her a microphone and Thay asks her to step forward and move to the center. She does this and begins to speak. At first I thought this was going to be some special recitation or song, perhaps to do with the coming of Tet. But quickly I see that is wrong. Her voice begins to falter, she bows and kneels, and while continuing to try to talk, she starts to cry. Although I cannot understand a word, it is heartbreaking to watch. Thay speaks for a long time in Vietnamese. He seems to be addressing the visiting nuns but it may be that he is simply looking straight ahead in their direction. Then in English he explains that this young nun has left the community without the permission of the Sangha, and now she is asking to return. He explains how it is all right for her to be angry with another monk or nun, or a group of monks or nuns, or even her teacher, but it is not permissible to be angry with the entire Sangha and leave. He reminds us all that the Sangha is one of the Three Jewels. Leaving in this manner causes worry and harm to the Sangha. He compares this action to a bird leaving the formation of its flock in flight. This puts the whole formation in jeopardy. Likewise this young woman has put the Sangha in danger. Then Thay kindly tells her this is a good time to return, a time of beginning anew, and she is dismissed.

This is so uncomfortable to watch. It feels like a public humiliation, but there is great wisdom in the Sangha conducting its business within the group and not behind closed doors. Later, when inquiring about the situation to a long term resident, I am told that this young nun has a willful nature and stubborn streak so the ceremony is seen as particularly helpful for her. I too can be willful, proud and stubborn like many Irish. I wonder if I could have stood up and taken Thay's correction. I wonder if I could manage the failure of that experience, and learn from it.

Friday, February 4

This morning meditation goes well. Yes, here I am still caught in the trap of judging, evaluating, measuring. But at this particular time, I am able to enjoy sitting quietly and peacefully through the inevitable distractions that arise. The short walk to meditation in the cool air of the early morning darkness wakes me up just enough to sit and yet the mind has not been overly stimulated by the surroundings. For me morning meditation has always been easier to enter than meditation at other times of the day. The stone walls of the hall are lit by just the altar candles and one small, red candle positioned on the floor at the opposite end of the zendo. Today I feel at home on my cushion. All is spacious. Time becomes indistinct. Before me is a sign in calligraphy, probably done by Thay, that reminds me I am a manifestation, not a creation. This sign is becoming a source of reflection as the days go on. In my Christian faith I was always taught that I am the creation of God, who has a personal relationship with me. What a mind boggling concept it is, that each and every one of us is chosen to exist by God. It speaks beautifully and directly to the uniqueness and sacredness of human life. The idea of manifestation is that we always exist, but now our form is our current body and mind. With our death we will not truly die, we will alter and manifest again in another form. So nothing truly expires. If a piece of paper is burned, it gives heat, ash, and smoke. The paper is gone but other realities appear. For me, the great beauty of this teaching is found in the realization that all is sacred. Every single thing is connected to other factors in the interdependence of animals, vegetables, and minerals. The necessary conclusion is that all, animate and inanimate, must be treated with reverence. There is a great challenge to the call of this teaching.

I do find myself strangely resistant to fitting in here at times, and then I'm sad, disappointed and hurt when I feel I don't belong. This experience is not limited to Plum Village, but here it can be clearly seen. Is it my need to distinguish myself from any group, even negatively? Is it my inability to commit? Is it my strongly stubborn and resistant nature that won't accept restrictions from others? Do I so need to feel some control? There is much to reflect on if I am ever to understand myself. And there is a need to approach myself in loving kindness as I find these darker aspects of myself. It is comforting to think of Thay's teaching about the seeds of consciousness. Within us all there are seeds for every possible emotion, belief or action. What is important is how we water our seeds; that we encourage the more positive ones to grow and flourish and that we let the negative ones lie dormant. This teaching is a great equalizer for me. No matter how bad a person may seem, I can picture that good lies somewhere within, but it has received no nourishment. And no matter how much a person may seem the hero, or heroine, I know that there are struggles beneath the surface from time to time, as the negative seeds are held in check. As Thay says, he is the starving child in Uganda, and he is the gunrunner. He is the refugee on a boat, and he is the pirate. And so it is, for us all. This teaching is so clarifying, again and again, for all the experiences of daily life.

I have the luck to clean Red Candle Meditation Hall again this morning. Alone and truly happy, every movement takes on a gentle rhythm and I feel the presence of the Buddha, touching my own Buddha nature within. These moments are to be cherished but not clung to, for all is passing. So then it is on to other tasks, and as I work with the others I begin to feel that push to prepare for the upcoming festivities. Tet celebrations begin here today at three o'clock, and go through Monday. The other Hamlets will be joining us, so there is a lot of work. My assignment is to move sitting cushions and chant books from Red Candle to the large meditation hall. A young physician, who is here on retreat to relieve the stress in her life, joins me. We use a wheelbarrow to pile the zafus and zabutons in high teetering towers and move them from hall to hall. At the large zendo a nun asks me to mop, so I get right to it since my skills in this area are really building. Another nun comes in and says not to mop — just as I am about to finish. This is confusing, as

I point out, and later she apologizes. It also has a rather comedic air, if one allows. Confusion is all just part of the natural fervor to prepare a memorable holiday and I am sure it is going to be one. The meditation hall looks just wonderful with a small, indoor flower garden carefully arranged, a New Year's tree of winter's branches with red envelops, another tree with yellow blossoms, red banners hanging, and everything spic and span.

Because the dining room is being prepared for the evening, we eat our lunch outside picnic style. All is still silent except for the messages of the bells, but it is nice to be out in the fresh air. It remains muddy from the rain but today the air is cool and clear, really lovely. After an hour break we go back to work and keep at it right up to the arrival of our guests.

When Thay arrives we gather in front of the main buildings for New Year's greetings. We form a loose circle with the Vietnamese speakers all in the center at Thay's request. He speaks about the significance of Tet. This is his 34th year in exile, and Thay's description of New Year's in Vietnam reveals a glimpse of the personal cost of his displacement. At this time in Vietnam all is being readied, just like in Plum Village. All the activity of cleaning and cooking, the hustle and bustle, is the same. His memories are of watermelons selling for very cheap prices as shops close at this late hour. One young Vietnamese nun sheds tears quietly, and Thay teases her in French. As we prepare for walking meditation, Thay tells his countrymen and women that they must take one step here and one step in Vietnam, not just walk in Vietnam. It feels a bit like listening in on a family's private conversation. But isn't that why I came in winter, to get closer to the heart of this family? And I feel the generosity that is implicit in the ease of this sharing of community, and I am deeply grateful.

Thay leads us in walking meditation. We walk around the lotus pond and many of us stop to look at the frogs displaying their antics. At times during walking meditation, especially on bright, sunny days, there is a lot of communication within the group, albeit nonverbal. At other times, it is as if each is a solitary figure within a moving cluster. Another reflection of the paradoxical nature of our existence. At the lovingly prepared zendo, we sing the Three Refuges in Vietnamese and English. One of the brothers leads us in practice for a while first and a new friend tells me that Thay had the men prepare the Vietnamese version earlier in Upper Hamlet. The story is that a lot of fun was had up there with Thay and the monks. In the end we sound wonderful, but maybe that's because I don't understand Vietnamese.

Thay reassures everyone that although we are apart from our families, we are together now as a spiritual family of brothers and sisters. This is an opportunity to be grateful we are together in this moment. Certainly this is a lot easier for us who are not missing Tet as our traditional holiday, but true none-the-less. And here again is the reminder to live in the present moment, to be always mindful, a constant practice that is one of the keystones of Buddhism.

Thay explains to us the parallel sentences that are in the hall. He says that in Vietnam calligraphers make these to sell so people can hang them in their homes on Tet. They are done on red paper with black ink just like the ones that are in front of us. Prepared in pairs, they hang beside doors or windows. It used to be they were written in Sino-Vietnamese but then the people could not read them so the calligraphers went out of business. Businesses continued to fail until the calligraphers changed to the popular modern languages of Vietnamese, French, and English. This made me think of all the work Thay does to make Buddha's teachings available through many languages and in a style relevant to today's world. His teaching is like a modern parallel sentence – profound, understandable and poetic.

The sentences are hanging in each of the hamlets for New Year's. In Lower Hamlet the first side is translated as: The year is new. The century is new. The millennium is new. The Sangha body vows to begin anew. On the second side the matching banner may be translated as: The

Patriarchs love us. The Bodhisattvas love us. The Buddhas love us. The noble community learns to love also.

Meditation follows and all the monastics are wearing their formal robes in a profusion of shades of yellow and orange. A large standing drum and the bell accompany us. It is a breathtaking delight of sight and sound. Our dinner is a great success and then we return to the hall for entertainment. What a change of pace! We all dissolve in laughter as a group of young monks from Upper Hamlet sing about the first ten years of being a monk. The lyrics are set to the tune of "Que Sera Sera", and get wittier with each verse. Next is a short play about the noble young Vietnamese prince who originated earth cakes as a New Year's tradition. Another play has an abbess choosing her successor from four promising young students and in the end choosing them all, plus a layperson. (Thay's vision of the future perhaps?) The Lower Hamlet nuns shift the mood again as they deliver some serious, beautiful songs. In the last play, the kitchen gods from each hamlet, and one from a mindfulness practice center, report their progress to the year 2000. Great show altogether!

At the end of the day I check in with the Bible. Just before the miracle of the loaves and fishes, Jesus takes his disciples off to rest with him. In this brief passage we get an image of Jesus leading his men away from the crowds. In the midst of all their activity and the mission so central to their lives, Jesus sees the need for rest, for prayer and reflection. Here in this small phrase, we find a common concern over space and time. How do we balance a life of active ministry and a life of prayer? Doing all in mindfulness must be the answer, but no easy accomplishment.

Saturday, February 5

Today we go to New Hamlet and meet in the striking meditation hall with its deep, vibrant purple carpet and fieldstone walls. The focus of the room is the serene image of Buddha made of what appears to be reddish-brown clay. It is similar to the lovely one outside the large meditation hall in Lower Hamlet, and probably done by the same artist.

We sit for about a half hour and then Thay arrives. This morning really seems to celebrate him. There is chanting, and then gifts of flowers and a picture are presented to him with best wishes expressed in the three languages of Plum Village. The goals of the Sangha to live together in joy, compassion and harmony are stated. It is noted that this would bring health and happiness to Thay. One of the senior nuns from Vietnam gives a greeting and then some small fireworks are lit. The monastics remain for a service called Touching the Earth and the rest of us leave. Those of us from Lower Hamlet are enjoying being the guests today!

Later we are called back for oracle reading. This is so intriguing and goes on for many hours. It is high-spirited, yet serious. First a name is called. That chosen person goes mindfully down the center aisle between the two sides of the assembled community. After bowing he, or she, sits before Thay and asks a question, any question at all. One hand is placed on the large bell; the person is instructed to breathe mindfully and choose a red envelope from inside the bell. In the envelope is a number. This number represents the verse of an epic poem by a famous Vietnamese writer. The two lines are chanted and then interpreted by two monastics, often a monk and a nun. Then Thay gives the final word on the meaning of the poetry, and how it relates to the question asked. The first line of the verse concerns the practice and the second line concerns the fruit of the practice. There is a final chant and the recipient bows twice and then backs part way down the aisle before mindfully returning to his or her place. Thay jokes with us that in Vietnam you have to pay for oracle readings, but here in Plum Village they are free!

It seems that the people selected for this first session of oracle reading, were carefully chosen to represent the groups in the community. Young, old, monastic, lay, American, French and Vietnamese are all quickly presented. Of course all of us listen with great interest to the questions and responses and gain from the teachings presented. For me, two of the most moving responses are to nuns who ask about all the suffering in their lives. Thay tells the first that she has to meditate on her suffering and remember that those who cause it also suffer. The second, he encourages to look deeply at her suffering in meditation. He suggests that she look not outside of herself for the cause of suffering, but look within to her mind and perceptions. He tells her to embrace her suffering and she will find it is a creation of her mind and she may come to understand that it is not reality itself. She will be free. In my own life I am sure that this is true of much suffering I have experienced. It certainly takes a lot of discipline to move from that urge to look outward for causes to blame, to moving inward with love to examine ourselves. It is equally difficult to surrender what, and whom, we love. When I have encountered great loss, through death or separation, the pain is only eased by recognizing the attachment in those feelings. Then I recall all is change and must be released. My heart fills with gratitude for the time given with the beloved and gratitude eases the suffering.

On the way home to Lower Hamlet, I ride with some other laypersons and we stop at the villages of Dumas and Allemans in search of a pharmacy. These are marvelous towns, so old, with narrow streets of businesses and homes oozing European charm. We visit a very old church that dates back to the 10th or 11th century. Our driver is a well-to-do Parisian matron who shows us the small hotel where she often stays before going to Plum Village. She rests up there before diving into the life of the community. Well, if only I had had that idea I could have avoided my teary arrival!

This is the first time I have strayed from the community for even a second, and it has been fascinating but I am equally happy to be going home to my Peacock Room in Persimmon Hall. Now I am resting and catching up on this journal as we prepare to celebrate Tet again tomorrow.

"Rising very early before dawn, he left and went off to a deserted place, where he prayed." (Mark 1:35) In the Gospel today we find Jesus slipping off for prayer in solitude. This happens between the working of miracles, in particular the curing of Simon's mother-in-law and the casting out of demons, and setting off to preach. In the midst of action Jesus seeks the support of spiritual reflection. And so my thoughts go again to this theme of Jesus' life of prayer supporting his work, supporting him.

Yesterday at Persimmon we woke up to find we had no electricity, so no heat or hot water. This made this morning's warm room and shower especially delightful. These days I slip into my sun salutations as smoothly as falling silk. First it seemed like such a limited, and limiting, yoga practice but it has become deeper and deeper, rhythmic and meditative. I feel like a sleek, warm cat stretching in the sun. And most days I am not warm, and never sleek or a cat! No breakfast or sitting meditation this morning since we are headed straight to Thay's Dharma talk in Upper Hamlet. As we settle in Still Water Meditation Hall, a special phone is set up so we can be joined by two Australian Sanghas, one in Sidney and one in Brisbane. These are small groups of about thirty people each. With great good cheer each one greets Thay for the New Year with song. Thay is delighted and teases them about choosing music that isn't from Plum Village. It is chilly, and my feet search for the bottom of my long coat to tuck into for warmth. Thay is holding his tea in both hands, undoubtedly also seeking the comfort of heat. Then we all settle in for a spellbinding Dharma talk.

Thay opens with his thoughts on the New Year. This is a time of hope for more peace and more happiness. Buddha is present right here and now and so we begin to practice anew in a profound and stable manner. The Buddha of love is the future Buddha, the Buddha of Tet. We are called to practice boundless love, and that love in our hearts will make our hearts suffer less.

Thay explains how the Buddha offers methods to help us keep love alive. We are fearful when we don't know our way. Our path is to understand deeply and love, even loving what is most difficult. Following the path of Buddha we know how to act. We are no longer in darkness, and confusion and anxiety are gone. Loving is kept joyful as we give happiness and remove suffering.

Equanimity means letting go, to practice no discrimination, to not be partial, to have no attachment. We have a tendency to love who is lovable but the person who is not lovable, needs our love more. If you love someone because the person is like you in religion, in nationality, or whatever, it is not really love. You cannot support only your own children. Rather you must share time, energy, and material resources with those who need you, and not ask for anything in return. We need equanimity in our love. Our goal is to try to relieve suffering through love; joy is secondary.

Thay continues by speaking about war. Certainly in his life he has learned to look deeply at this tragic human experience. He tells us that during a war both sides need love, even if one is stronger. If you think that one side is evil, don't be so sure. There is suffering on both sides. In South Africa, everyone understood the suffering of Blacks, but the White people also suffered.

The challenge is to keep a lot of space in your heart. Feel detached but with a lot of love. So love, Thay tells us, but allow freedom for the other person. Then when you love someone that person will have a lot of space around him or her, a gift of liberty. We must love in such a way that both sides have a lot of joy and peace. Thay believes we need training in this. When you love someone you don't vow to enter prison. You don't want to be someone's prisoner, even if the prison is love. The prison palace of love is a very dangerous trap. If we are caught in it, we will suffer all our lives. The guards suffer also. This is true for two partners, for parents and children, and for friends. Parents must not impose their views on their children, even their ideas of happiness. All must go in their own direction.

You may want to divorce your parents or your children, but the attachment is too large. You may feel loving is so difficult it is better not to love. That is a tragedy. If your views are different from each other's, listen with a refreshed mind. Maybe new insights will be learned. It is the same with a student and teacher. Thay tells us the door of his heart is always open. Envision the full moon in an empty sky and provide a lot of space. The power of a king and the royal palace could not deprive Siddhartha of liberty. He is the king of liberty, love, and space.

The Dharma talk continues with instruction on suffering. Usually when you suffer you want the other person to suffer too. This goes back and forth and escalates the difficulty. With the path of love, compassion and understanding, the situation can change drastically. Ask if you are following the path of the Buddha and bodhisattvas. Do your thinking, words and action reflect them? To love is an art. You need to train yourselves. Looking deeply for only a few minutes may relieve you of a burden that has been weighing on your heart for years.

There may be sleepless nights when your heart feels cut by a sword. Another has been unfair to you, has betrayed you. Go on the path of understanding and love for all holy persons, the path of beauty and goodness. Observe your words, acts and looks. If your look is ugly it will make others suffer too. Ask yourself if you are still on the path of compassion and loving-kindness, or if you have gone astray.

Thay finishes by reminding us of the chapter on Avalokita in the Lotus Sutra. Avalokita is the universal door; she is love born in us. We are told that compassion is like powerful thunder, and loving-kindness is like a gentle cloud. When the thunder and cloud come together they are transformed into rain, the rain of the Dharma that extinguishes all afflictions.

The beauty and power of this Dharma talk stay with us as we begin walking meditation. At the New Year it is traditional in Vietnam and in Plum Village, to visit people in their homes. So we will begin visiting each other in our rooms today. This is the only time each year that the monastics open their rooms to others. For us few visitors, this tradition is introduced by Thay leading us to his residence during the walking meditation. Just off the main area of Upper Hamlet, we walk down some steps to a simple wooden cabin situated on a hillside. The cabin, called Sitting Still Hut, has a deck area that extends around it so we are able to stand together and look at the view. One of the nuns tells me that the cabin had been prepared for our visit because it usually isn't so neat. There is a tiny room with an altar holding tangerines and earth cakes for Tet. On the wall hangs a picture of Thay at age sixteen when he became a monk. There is a little oriental style carpet on which his cushion rests, and about the room are audiotapes, and other odds and ends, that give this small home a lived-in feeling. Everyone lines up to look in the window as if we might get some kind of inspiration, insight or blessing through the brief sharing of this personal space. We do not see Thay's bedroom, which I would guess contains his writing area, but the sister tells me it is very monastic in style. I feel this hospitality is generous of Thay. I wonder if he ever tires of this curiosity about him. The community does seem to make a concerted effort to protect him from excessive activity or distracting interruptions. Certainly he is a scarce and treasured resource for this world.

At lunch today I sit with a warm, engaging, American man who is a minister and father to one of the new young nuns. He has been visiting the community for several months, coming for her ordination and staying on to practice with the community for several months. He is such a testimony to what fatherhood can be. Then we go for the continuing oracle reading.
Here are a couple of examples.

A man from the local community receives verse 115.
"Surrounded by the openness of nature in the four directions,
I'd like to bow to convey my gratitude for the great merit I have received."
This was interpreted as meaning that boundaries are within us. The Three Refuges, or Three

Jewels, give a lot of space and peace. Our hearts and minds are opened and the Sangha protects us. True freedom comes from taking refuge in our ancestors, our motherlands and seeing our true selves. It comes from our family roots and our spiritual roots.

An American woman receives verse 4.
"Now we see each other very clearly.
Practicing is the best way. Attachment is not good."
The interpretation suggests that some attachment is getting in the way of her practice. It is a love, but not the kind spoken of by Thay in the Dharma talk. She is not yet ready to give it up.

After some hours of oracle readings we go on to visit rooms. With one of my roommates I visit the lay section of Upper Hamlet. This is a male bastion, but some couples appear to reside here also. Upstairs in one of the old buildings there is a suite of rooms comprised of a large common room ringed by bedrooms crowded with bunk beds. A big, wooden table greets us at the top of the stairs with a feast of goodies: cookies, candies, nuts, fruit, tea, etc. Inside, cushions are invitingly arranged in a circle and we eat, chat and sing some folk songs. Everyone is enjoying the camaraderie, and we could have stayed forever, but it is time to go on to the monks' rooms. We visit one with two young monks, a Vietnamese and an American. They have a simple, charming space arranged. The tea is wonderful and served with nuts and fruit. Each tells his story of joining the order with a lot of laughs, and sighs for lost girlfriends and shocked families.

We walk back down to Lower Hamlet for a light supper, short break and then the task of chopping vegetables for the 160 Tet celebrants expected tomorrow. I am getting very skilled with a knife! There will be no trouble sleeping tonight. A new roommate has arrived so there are four in Peacock now. She is a real beauty, a German artist who lives in Paris and has been to Plum Village many times.

It has been a glorious day. There is ease in the community now, as if we are assured the celebration will be a success, and all are settling in to enjoy it. Smiles greet us at every turn; there is more easy conversation, and a loving, festive atmosphere envelops all.

It rained again last night. This morning's sitting is optional so we are fewer than usual. There is a stillness and calm in the zendo, and through my mind pass images and sounds of inspiring church experiences – Christmas altars, splendid European cathedrals, Latin chants at Benediction, etc. The most compelling is the memory of a Christmas mass at my son Chandan's, private elementary school. The young boys, in their natty uniforms of gray blazers, striped ties and navy slacks, filed into the church crowded with their families. Starting with the littlest, they walked single file up the aisles to the sound of one of their peer's perfect soprano voice singing "Once in Royal David's City." At the time, I was moved profoundly by the breathtaking beauty and glory of those innocents. Their shining faces and the haunting music remain before me now. The Divine finds many ways to reach us. Here, Tet seems to be evoking sacred memories in me. And then the peace and silence of emptiness.

We sit so long that I wonder if there is no nun leading us. If no bell rings what will happen? Will someone finally get up? Will we leave at the breakfast bell? In the end, the small zendo bell rings. There is a young nun who seems to have gotten lost in her own meditation. We continue with a slow walking meditation and then it's off to breakfast. It is our turn to receive visitors today at Lower Hamlet. The White Clouds set up the cushions in the large meditation hall and then I mop the muddy floors of Persimmon. My roommates and I straighten up our room for guests and decorate with simple arrangements from nature including evergreen branches, lotus pods, and rocks. We already have a good supply of cookies and then get a donation of great leftovers from the Upper Hamlet men we visited yesterday. It is simple but plentiful and pleasing. One of my current roommates is a young woman from Vietnam here with her husband. They are living in Europe and are glowing with happiness spending Tet here. It is a gift to be around all this joy. At 10 o'clock, when chores are done, the oracles begin again.

It would seem that we might get tired of the oracle readings but they continue to fascinate us. People ask all kinds of questions: what foods to eat, can the practices of Plum Village transfer to Vietnam, how to handle particular relationships, and, of course how to practice the teachings of Buddha. Somehow the verses are always interpreted in a way that makes sense. Advice is given from the most esoteric to the mundane. One retreatant is reminded to sit straight during Dharma talks, and another is told not to eat hot peppers or sour pickles. A nun is told to open her heart to her daughter. Thay is not always present but often he stops in and contributes to the ceremony. I love it when he teases the faltering chanters that they must have missed breakfast, or that they have their own melodies. But his words of wisdom are helpful to all. He speaks of gratitude that is a form of deep love, responding to the good acts, favors and trust of others. He reminds us of the tree that brings out the leaves, and then the leaves fall and do their best to nourish the tree. The flowing goes both ways. Our lives have meaning by repaying the debts we owe to our families, our ancestors, our countries, and our spiritual ancestors. Our true purpose is to bring up the next generation in the best way we can and in a spirit of gratitude to the previous generation. Whatever vocation is chosen — politician, teacher, artist, etc., the young person must use it to express this gratitude. You can tell he has deep concern for the young of Vietnam, now over half of that population. He fears that they have no direction, and of course they need it to experience the fullness of life. The energy of faith needs to be nourished and kept alive so the happiness of the practice will spread, and the sun will rise in the country. Hope will rise.

One young European asks about her connection to herself. Thay notes that she has a path that is already deeply impressed on her but she keeps analyzing it. He advises her to listen with her heart. "You think, therefore you are not what you are." At other times I have heard him put this similarly with humor. "You think, therefore you are not." This is a message most of us in the West can use to balance our left-brained dependence on our mind consciousness. We are not complete without a deep integration of this dominant mind with our heart, body and spirit.

When it comes time to have my own oracle read, we have broken down into smaller groups to accommodate everyone. I actually find this more relaxed and wait to have Sister Chan Khong read mine. She has inspired me since the first time I saw her. She is Thay's right hand, the one who sees to all the practicalities, as well as a woman of great spiritual depth and public service. She takes the reading from me but before she looks at it she kindly asks about my family and if they support my practice. How lucky I am to be able to report that they are most extraordinary in this! She wants to know something about my life, so I tell her about my husband, my children, my work as a teacher, and about my journey to Buddhism. Her manner is so gentle, full of humor and kindness. She is incredibly beautiful to me.

The verse I have received is no 171.
"Your heart is full of love and gratitude.
The autumn moon has shone several times over you."

Sister tells me that this means I have already shown much love and gratitude but that I must continue to do so with my beloved ones and with others. It seems so simple and sweet to me at first. But then when I think of Thay's Dharma talk yesterday, I know that this simplicity and sweetness hold a great challenge. Loving is the most comprehensive and important goal of our lives — certainly not simple, and often not sweet. I never really need to have another oracle reading. This will be an aspiration before me forever.

After lunch we go visiting at the nuns' building, Purple Cloud. Their quarters are bright and inviting. Cozy beds are made on raised platforms that hold their mattresses; the platform tops open up to provide storage. Lots of snacks and tea are enjoyed, but most of all I love looking at the photo albums. Life stories are told in the treasured collections of images of family, friends, homes, ordinations and Thay. We don't linger long because we want to take a turn hosting and we need to open up our own room.

Somehow we make it look quite festive. All is straightened up neat and clean; candles are lit; nature is brought inside in simple arrangements; and a bounty of food tantalizes. People drop in, usually in ones and twos, and we indulge in long, personal conversations. But by far, the most fun is a large group of nuns and monks who arrive led by our cook. She is a small, wiry, older, Vietnamese nun, surely one of the senior nuns, and she packs the energy of a hundred monastics! What a treat to have her come. They all eat, and drink, and sing. Cameras come out and we tease as pictures are taken. There is great good cheer. What delight to hear raucous laughter ring in Persimmon!

After dinner two of my roommates and I choose not to visit, or host. We are so tired. Now we are flat out on our beds, happily in silence once again. I have no doubt that our cook is still making the rounds. Our interesting new roommate has mysteriously gone out and returns at an unknown hour.

Tuesday, February 8

Today Tet is over and we have a lazy day. Boy does it feel good! I have done laundry and although my whites are now a peculiar blue-gray, all is clean. The clothes are hanging in a drying room that is part of the attic of the main buildings. Getting there is a bit of an adventure. After climbing the wooden stairs, you are under the eaves with minimal lighting, uneven floors and the atmosphere of a Gothic novel. I wonder how long the drying will take since the intermittent rain continues. I am taking time to catch up on my writing, trying to remember everything accurately. And I have done my share of community work by cleaning up the kitchen and taking in the garbage cans. Tomorrow morning starts at 5 so it is good to have this little break.

Last night a man came to our door and gave me an envelope addressed to me with a poem from Thay. It is a verse written by Thay in 1960 and chosen for this New Year's greeting.

be the monarch of your life
and sign the decree
to exile suffering
and
call back from all points of the cosmos
the power of birds and flowers
the vitality of youth.
the whole universe will smile
when your eyes smile.

I know I will always be happy I came here. This experience will continue to unfold for me long after this time in Plum Village is over. But there is not a day I don't wish to leave also. This is a challenging place for me. There is no privacy – none at all. And the routine is highly structured. Both of these aspects of monastery life are difficult for me. There is a need to always follow the orders of your work family in the Sangha; and although in theory we can say no to tasks, it is just about impossible for me. Actually it seems to be that way for all the guests except perhaps the very young ones, of whom there are several. These cute girls can be seen ducking out of the meditation hall, and pleading illness as working meditation is assigned. Light and serious at the same time, they fill the Hamlet with their exuberant spirit. They make me smile and long for my students.

You have to really surrender yourself here. The individual is not recognized or catered to at all, and I realize that I am spoiled in that, and in many other ways. So Plum Village presents many lessons to me each day. Sometimes I benefit from them well, and sometimes barely. I am learning about myself, and my striving for recognition and support. I am also learning I can do without these usual gifts in my life. In fact they may not be gifts at all. I am surprised at how caught up in myself I seem to be, including all this analyzing of how I'm doing on retreat. The lessons go on and on.

This morning we have meditation in the large zendo. My mind is busy but I relax into it as time passes. I had nightmares last night -- making sandwiches very fast for work, feeling pressured, forgetting my son's birthday, he being devastated and I helpless with no explanation. I woke up so upset. Home is deeply missed and it is seeping into my dreams. I want to call, but to do this we need to use one of two public phones. To use them, the correct phone card is needed. That is available in the bookstore here, but it opens only erratically. It is just a tiny stone building with lots of Thay's books and a few other odds and ends of necessities and snacks. There is no schedule for opening it, so I just keep my eyes peeled. Not exactly Barnes and Noble!

The newer residence hall here, Plum Hill, has been without heat or hot water for four days. It is so wet the air seems colder than it is actually, so these poor women are walking around in parkas looking for a warm room, shower, or whatever. We lose our heat in Persimmon all the time but so far not for any long period. Thank the stars!

This morning we recite the Five Mindfulness Trainings and I get it right as far as the bowing goes. The Trainings are truly a gift in my life. Once again I feel such a strong response to the positive call of them, the "I will" instead of the "I won't."

My Thursday cooking duty begins today with two hours of julienning carrots. Then I skip walking meditation to move my still wet laundry from the drying attic to our room where it now soggily hangs. On to lunch, a short break, and a question/answer session with Sister Jina, our abbess. This is a time for guests to ask questions on the practice. We gather in the Red Candle Zendo and I have been happily anticipating this session because Sister has made a strong impression on me. Just observing her, one sees a warm and highly spiritual woman who is blessed with humility and humor. She is radiant. As we meet she is relaxed, reflective and caring in her answers and this is how I have seen her move through her days that must be full of demands and difficulties. As questions are asked she always encourages the group to respond, before responding herself. She talks about being a yoga teacher in one of her answers. Perhaps my own interest in yoga makes me feel a bond to her. Sister shares how she began meditating with others. She simply set the time and place and invited others. If they came that was fine and if they didn't, that was fine also. She just started. And they came.

I enjoy participating in the session but some of the longer-term guests don't participate much. At one bad moment I realize I am talking away and the phone is ringing. In Plum Village when the phone rings we treat it as a mindfulness bell and stop everything for three rings. Here I am rambling on right through it. Nothing like sitting there talking about meditation, unmindfully! I'd like to think I was so focused on speaking that I didn't hear it, but that may be a lame rationalization. Anyway, it is embarrassing. One of my fellow retreatants said she had learned something from my comments to a woman who was having difficulty settling into her sitting. There are a couple of visual imagery practices I learned from Thay, that I use regularly. One is of the glass of cloudy cider becoming clear as it sits. The other is a set of four images: a blooming flower, a strong, stable mountain, clear, calm, reflecting water, and open space. You identify yourself with these images and it can be a wonderful tool for arriving at a meditative state. Thay has written beautifully about many such skillful means.

After the question and answer session we go right to dinner and then I learn I have to cook after dinner. This means I will miss evening sitting and grumblings arise within me. I sit at the table waiting for instructions for half an hour after dinner and then the plan is changed. We will cook at 6am tomorrow instead. There will be no breakfast tomorrow because it is a Dharma talk morning, but luckily there still is a stash of cookies in our room. Earlier at the afternoon meeting we had been told we would have a guided meditation this evening, but we don't. We have two half hour sittings with walking meditation in between. I am happy to be in Red Candle whatever we are doing. The schedule has changed again so then we have announcements, a blip in our Noble Silence. Today there seems to be a lot of disorganization. It seems to be a teacher revealing some inflexibility in me. Oh, could that be so???

My new roommate has disappeared again! She is like a sprite! And here's good news – I got a phone card to call home!

Thursday, February 10

This morning my sprightly roommate is back and we go off to the kitchen at six to cook since she is also part of the White Cloud family. No morning meditation for us today since it is chop-chop time. One Vietnamese nun is there, but the rest of our team isn't, so there is nothing to do. We always wait for the person in charge of the meal for instructions. We sit and have tea and my new friend tells me about her budding romance with a retreatant from Upper Hamlet. That's where she has been going, to rendezvous! She is so delighted with this handsome hunk of a young man, and they are a picture-perfect Hollywood pair. When he wants to see her, he walks down to our hamlet and plays the piano that is in the main building. The music tells her he is there, and she goes to meet him. With her car they are able to get around as they wish. She is so happy it is contagious. Of course they must be breaking a million rules but that is not my business. Actually, here I'm not sure whose business that would be.

Our team arrives and after being reminded that it is Noble Silence, we go to work. I cook one large batch of zucchini and put some green beans in water. Actually we seem to be more in the way than anything this morning. Finally Sister tells us to come back at 3 or 4 in the afternoon to help with dinner. Dinner is always creatively rearranged leftovers so it is not a big chore. Soon Thay will arrive for the Dharma talk.

Our Dharma talks begin at 7:30 before breakfast. In Vietnam they are held at that hour to avoid the heat of the day. Heat is no problem here! As a matter of fact, it is not on in the main hall and I can feel my feet turning into blocks of ice. The men from Upper Hamlet start us off with a chant. One of them tells me they were just told they would sing this morning, so there wasn't much practice time. Actually they sound fine, a little low and slow like a lullaby. Maybe I'm sleepy.

Thay continues his reading of the Sutra text in French, Chinese, and Vietnamese and then gives some commentary. It is not easy to follow, but it is engaging. He is too, as he compares the translations done in different languages, and then with other traditions, and later developments. I don't worry about getting it all. In the past I have heard Thay say to just let the Dharma rain fall on you, and that is what I try to do as I listen. I have faith that what is necessary for my life will come to me. Here are some of the drops of Dharma rain that have come my way today.

Thay tells us there are three levels of penetration in the practice. The first is learning to listen deeply, the second is looking deeply and the third is putting your understanding into practice. I felt him speak to me as he said that beginners come with so many questions and an inability to listen. They want to hear what agrees with concepts they already possess. It is important to empty the mind so there is no judgment. Release all your knowledge. This is the prized "beginner's mind." Otherwise when you hear something, you think you already know it, and you don't listen to it deeply. Thay says if you read the <u>Lotus Sutra</u> several times every day, a year later you will still find something new. And although we may learn a lot, we may fail to put it into practice. Good instruction for bookworms like me who read about, rather than do, lots of things. When we share we are able to recognize our weak points and reach a deeper level of understanding. "I want to practice as a river, not a drop of water."

Once again Thay compares us to a TV set, today with twenty channels. Push the right channel and your Buddha nature appears. Let go of the less desirable channels of ourselves. He also uses another remarkable image for this same truth. The flamingo can drink from water mixed with milk and take only the milk.

This theme of interbeing continues as Thay talks about permeation: language and belief in selfhood. On language Thay speaks of words. If you think of "table", "heaven", "person", or whatever, your image will be different from those of others. They are only words. Then he speaks of selfhood by talking about babies. At first they cannot distinguish themselves from their mothers. Indeed, the words for mother in many languages start with the sound of "m." As we grow and see ourselves as separate we become proud and arrogant with success, and desperate in failure.

Nothing is totally collective and nothing is totally individual. The balance depends on conditions. Several examples are given. In Vietnam girls wear the traditional, long, graceful ao dai, and Thay was shocked when he first saw the mini ao dai. But after some months it was possible for him to see the beauty. Paris is reality for all the French but it is different for a Parisian, compared to a person from elsewhere in France. Our communities condition our opinions about beauty, ethics, etc. All flowers show some collective elements but also have some individual differences. It is the same for feelings such as anger or shame. The sun is very collective, but in Vietnam people do not like it and in France we do. In Vietnam people love a cloud, but here they do not. The laws are the same for all but if you know how to use them, they protect and if you don't, they oppress. Your eyes are yours, but if you drive a bus they are collective. Just ask the passengers.

We have a long meditation walk and come back to the dining room to wait for lunch. Thay goes through a couple of times, once checking the food as he walks the length of the serving table. People bow as he walks past, and of course, I do too. Thank goodness, I'm getting better at the details. I am a bit apart from the others, standing toward the center of the crowded room as we wait. Thay pauses, turns, smiles and bows to me. I am charmed to my toes!

"You disregard God's commandment but cling to human tradition." Jesus is speaking to the Pharisees but later, in a similar vein, to his disciples. As I read, I wonder what he would say to us today if he walked the earth as man. What is the essential set of beliefs for a Christian? Think of the variety of answers one would get to that question if every Christian responded. My answer? For a long time what has made the most sense to me is the Old Testament commandment to love God, and then John's account of the new commandment given by Jesus. "I give you a new commandment: love one another. Just as I have loved you, you also must love one another. By this love you have for one another, everyone will know that you are my disciples." (John 13: 34-35) I would like to believe that the intent was for all people to love one another, not just the Christian community. But too often Christians think of themselves as "the chosen." The natural result of this thinking is that if God has chosen some, he has not chosen others. It leads to a dangerous kind of superiority complex that strikes me as un-Christ like.

I believe that an understanding of the divine nature of life came to us through Jesus. It is a treasure in my heart because it is my heritage and the initial spiritual experience of my life. It is how I touched the Divine as a child. As an adult I have strived to be a good Christian, as my understanding unfolds. For me the good Christian is all-embracing. After the fundamental caring of self, she puts others first. She brings an understanding nature to all, even those she finds difficult to accept. She sees the Kingdom of God in all aspects of life around her, both positive and negative. Indeed, she sees all of creation as the expression of the Divine.

It seems clear to me that revelation has come to humankind through many messengers at many points in time. All spiritual traditions and searching must be valued. Exploring Buddhism has only strengthened this belief. I feel as though I lived in a room with a spectacular view through a large picture window, and now a second window has been opened that brings a new perspective and deeper understanding, making all experience richer and more splendid. How blessed I am, and how I wish this good fortune could be everyone's!

Friday, February 11

Last night two of my roommates packed to leave today. The third continued her romance by staying out until two, saying good-bye to her departing lover. I was so tired at meditation this morning that I had a hard time staying awake. I did yoga eye movement exercises to save me. It's a good thing we were facing the wall, or it would have been quite a distracting show for any wandering gazes. But finally peace comes to my cushion and images of lost loved ones flicker in my mind – touches felt, breath felt, laughter heard, glorious eyes shining. Silence.

Our Abbess was inviting the bell and went over our usual time by about a half hour. It is interesting how the body clock gets set so easily. I can tell the minute we are over the schedule, and on a day like today, it makes me restless. I feel like the sitting is so long. Now if the sitting period was set for two hours, and we ended at the same time, I would feel no strain. Perhaps I would even feel incomplete. It is fascinating to observe the powerful internalization of this clock we live by.

The morning is quieter than usual so I manage to clean the room well in preparation for the new guests. Floors are mopped, beds made, everything dusted and garbage taken out. I even have time to scrub myself up. I will miss my departing roommates. Although there is not a lot of interaction, there is an intimacy derived from sharing space with people this way. Even during Noble Silence, there is communication and we learn about each other in small ways. Of course at times we chat and have enjoyable, relaxing breaks. And, truth be told, at times there are whispered conversations during Noble Silence. Neighbors hit the walls as reminders if it is too much for anyone. Some of the retreatants come with no Buddhist background. A couple of my roommates have never read anything by Thay. Others are frequent visitors and have a great deal of knowledge, not just about Thay's work, but also about this community. Some are practicing Buddhists, some are spiritual seekers, some are just curious. It is interesting to meet everyone. What I really long for is more interaction between the monastics and the lay visitors. There is little opportunity to have any meaningful conversations, much less instruction, here. The learning that takes place is accomplished by joining the practice. For me, this is the primary spiritual experience and the time here is a unique opportunity, but it would be well augmented by having a type of spiritual advisement process for retreatants, at least for those who would like to have that sharing and guidance. It could be that they don't have enough monastics prepared as Dharma teachers to take on such a role at this time.

The next two days are at Upper Hamlet and I find myself relieved that I will be able to walk back and forth as I like. At New Hamlet, where we are dependent on car rides, we don't have this freedom. I continue to observe this need for independence within myself. I do not want to be under any authoritative control and I cherish time alone. As I look deeply at my emotions I think these feelings stem from a highly structured and monitored childhood. As an adult I want to determine as much as I can about my environment and my activities. That is part of why teaching is a comfortable profession for me. It offers a lot of autonomy and especially so at my particular high school.

The monastery is nourishing to me; I am refreshed watching the monks and nuns in the rhythm of their daily lives. Meaningful freedom can only be found within, and here I can seek that and learn from the search. There are places here that I will treasure always – Red Candle Zendo, a little niche in the wall in Persimmon that holds a Buddha, and the enchanting, serene Buddha in the garden outside the large meditation hall. This Buddha can be enjoyed sitting outside, or through the enormous window in the sheltering zendo. The old stone walls and warmth of wooden beams, the smells of burning logs, candles and incense, the rub of a friendly cat and the touch of a bamboo breeze, all fill my heart and feed my spirit. But I know this could not be a happy, permanent way of life for me – at least the "me" of today. The bells, and the bows, and all the small rituals would soon cease to be comfortable and I would long for the privacy and open road of my life.

Walking meditation is revelatory today. For the first time I really touch the magic of it. My feet are in contact with the ground, but the motion induces a real meditative state as I slowly walk through the woods. I am aware of the group but feel somehow alone, not at all connected to them. It is a long walk and within the woods is a muddy stream. We stop at the banks and gaze into the stream. My meditative state abruptly leaves me and I look at this brown water wondering why we are doing this. There is nothing beautiful about this water. It certainly is not blue, or clear, or rippling or attractive in any way. I see no trace of life in it, no fish swimming or plants moving. But simply because the others are, I keep looking at the stream; I am a part of this Sangha. All of a sudden my awareness shifts and I see, not the water, but the reflection of the woods in it. Magnificent trees behind me spread their images in the water before me. The muddy water becomes a picture of majesty and beauty and I think of Thay's teaching on Thursday. The dirty water always contains the pure water.

Today will be the Dharma Lamp Transmission ceremony when Thay initiates new Dharma teachers. The weather is frosty, and car windows have to be scraped before we can leave for Upper Hamlet. As we settle into the large meditation hall at Upper Hamlet, there is much anticipation. Most of the retreatants, myself included, have never seen this ceremony so it is a special opportunity for us. There is a lot of good cheer in the air. Smiling Sister Jina walks to her seat with her folded Sanghati robe balancing on her head looking like a third world woman on her way to the market. Cool abbess! When all are gathered, Thay begins.

Alone Thay chants, invites the bell, and lights the incense. Then the wooden bell is invited and all the monks and nuns join in the chanting. The sounds bring a sacred solemnity to the hall. The large Dharma lamp is lit and placed beside Thay and as the dawn lightens the sky, the veil of frost on the windows slowly dissolves from the edges, inward.

Each new Dharma teacher goes before Thay with two fellow monastics and presents a gatha, a short poetic saying that assists the practice of mindfulness. Thay then chants, the others touch the earth, and a smaller version of Thay's lamp is given to the new teacher. Then the little procession of three goes around the back of Thay's platform to the other side of the hall and the new teacher takes his, or her, place on a lower platform to present a talk. This talk is primarily a reflection on experiences with Buddhism and feelings about this new role.

The ceremonies go on all day but I only stay for the first two. Then I walk through the beautiful countryside by myself and return to Lower Hamlet. The day is crisp and clear, and feelings of joy reverberate through each step. The ceremony is a demonstration of the healthy growth of this blessed Sangha. May it go on and on and on through time as the teachings transform all they touch. In America there is such a need for this practice of mindfulness to relieve the intense stress of daily living. To stop, to look deeply, would bring crashing down the gods of materialism, greed, violence and addiction that plague us. I remember my young Vietnamese-American students and pray especially for them. So many have already rejected so much of their heritage, including, and perhaps especially, their spiritual heritage. It was this rejection that led me to a deeper study of Thay, hoping to help them find the values in their tradition. Whatever else was accomplished, my own life was transformed. And I continue to hold these beloved students in my heart.

While teaching in China last summer, I visited a number of temples. Some were deserted; the only evidence of people came from the paper currency thrown before images of Buddhas considered bearers of good luck, prosperity, or fertility. Other temples had a theme park atmosphere and as people holidayed, they picnicked on the grounds and romped through the park-like properties. One even had a water park with pool, waterslides, concession stands, etc. Not a single person at prayer and only an occasional monk could be seen in the background. Chinese friends tell me that it is different in the countryside where there are more practicing Buddhists, but in the temples I visited there was a hollowness of spirit.

At a museum for Confucius in Beijing, there is a little souvenir shop. There in the back, on the bottom shelf of a display cabinet, were tossed some small stone heads. I asked to see them. They were Buddha or Bodhisattva images taken from destroyed temples during the Cultural Revolution. I knew I might not be able to get them home but I decided to try to take two out. Right away I wanted to lift them from their dirty heap and find them a place of reverence. Luckily they made it and they are now at home, admired and honored.

But poor China. So successfully Communist that religion is still looked down upon, especially by the young. In my introduction of myself to my students there, I always showed them pictures to give them glimpses of my American life. When they saw pictures of my church and Thay, these beautiful young people gasped and, at times, giggled. What was once theirs is so foreign to them now. So much to pray for, so many to remember, my heart blesses them all as I realize my own grace in this sacred place – in this present moment, this wonderful moment.

Back home at Lower Hamlet I call home and am so delighted to reach Tom. I have been looking forward to taking the opportunity for days and luckily he is home. We have a long conversation about the mundane housekeeping details of life and it delights my heart.

Both of my roommates are around. One never went to Upper Hamlet, and the other returned soon after I did. But there are only a few people in the hamlet so it is quiet and restful. For me, yesterday and today have been the first totally relaxed days here. I am enjoying living out of my small suitcase. It is so gloriously simple compared to the complexities of running a household of four. It is also easier to be mindful in a world of limited possessions and distractions. A lesson to pack when I leave Plum Village!

We return to Upper Hamlet for Thay's Dharma talk today on the Mahayana text he has been presenting. The Lotus Bud Sangha from Sidney has joined us again. The sutra is quite difficult and at one point Thay teases the Australians by asking if they think they are wasting their phone money on something so hard to understand.

In a very similar vein to the last theme in the Dharma talk on the collective and the individual, this one is about the common and the specific. Thay tells us a cloud can look like many different things to different people, depending on their perceptions. Another example is of a table. For a person it is used for writing or eating, but for a termite it is food. A river we may use to wash our clothes, is a palace for the fish. Nothing is only individual or specific, and nothing is only common or collective. Collective manifestation is difficult to transform because it is such a huge reality. It is so huge we can see only a part of it.

Thay teaches us that through practice we are able to transform negativity. We feel the world wc experience is ugly in some way. Perhaps people are cruel. Things may seem impure and sad, but through practice you are able to change your perception and you realize that all is beautiful. Everything is a wonder. You have a holy, relaxed, free view of the Kingdom of God, the Pure Land.

If you have Buddha eyes, the Kingdom of God is holy because you are a holy person.

He goes on to talk about manifestation. I think of the words that face me in the Red Candle Hall where I sit each morning. "You are not a creation. You are a manifestation." According to this teaching nothing is created and nothing is destroyed. Thay holds up his hand and says what we see are his five fingers. They are manifested. What we can't see are the unmanifested things, like his abilities to create poetry and calligraphy. If the conditions are sufficient, if the paper and ink are present, then we would see the poetry and calligraphy.

We tend to be caught in a particular form of manifestation. We think the form we know is the only one worthwhile. We can be found in other forms, so we need to do better. If we can recognize the one we love in different manifested forms, we are not caught in grief, suffering and despair. We are not subjected to birth and death. We need to practice a way of looking at the ones we love in other forms. On retreats I have heard Thay talk to parents who have lost children and comfort them with this teaching. How nearly impossible it must be for them to be comforted! Perhaps for some, this can transform the pain.

Thay tells the story of his mother having a miscarriage the year before he was born. He says he wondered for a long time if he was his brother.

He came to the conclusion that he is. The time was not appropriate, the conditions not sufficient, for him to be born earlier.

Buddha was not the property of his parents, the king and the queen. He became a collective object for all of mankind. We can recognize him anywhere, anytime. Buddha is always available to you if you are free from discrimination and attachment.

Speaking about his own future, Thay asks that his disciples not cry when his current manifestation ends. If they practice they will be prepared. Thay notes that the Tibetans expect a new manifestation of their teachers three or four years after their deaths. In Plum Village it is different. Already Thay sees other manifestations of his life in some disciples, in his books and in poems, and these manifestations will continue to do his work. So there is no need to cry when one manifestation is gone.

Thay teaches on mental constructions by telling the famous old story of the snake and the rope. In the twilight you walk and panic when you see a snake. You almost scream. This experience comes from your stored consciousness. Someone brings a light and you see it is only a rope. The snake is a mental construction. The rope is reality because it can be touched. But if you look deeply into the rope you will see that it is tree fibers, electrons, space and not a rope at all.

Next, Thay addresses interdependence, or dependent co-arising, and explains that when we truly see this we will have no fear. In this teaching elements rely on each other to manifest. They come together and they dissolve. For example, in films it is light and color we see; there is no real actor on the screen. What we see is an optical illusion. We are laughing and crying at a mirage. We have to train ourselves to see the objects and subjects of transmissions, to transcend our attachments and to see the co-arising of various conditions.

Complete reality is as it is. We see only a part of it. If we are angry with someone for ten years we think she is a snake. Then we find out she is only a rope!

Thay speaks a while longer about dependent co-arising. The ideas are so beautiful to contemplate. Here we realize that the existence of anything depends on other elements. All is related, intertwined. To understand, you look for patterns. The right arises because of the left. Above is present because of below. If there is no below, there is no above. Thay draws a diagram of the elements that comprise a rainbow and as he does so, I watch him and think of all the elements that have helped him manifest and then of all the elements that have connected us in this flow of ideas. And now the flow is continuing through other elements. As we begin to understand that we are not separate, we can be comforted. Beyond comfort, we can experience profound joy and freedom. There is such a strong tendency toward isolation in American society today; this teaching brings healing. For me, to experience the oneness of all is like a kiss from the universe.

Thay continues on with his talk by discussing consciousness and science. I am lost much of the time, or perhaps just full and I try to let the Dharma rain fall. There is such a tendency to feel I'm missing something, a feeling of opportunity lost, when things are not clear to me. Luckily Thay is such a good teacher that this doesn't happen often. But beyond that, how much more do I need to learn? Is it necessary to attack all the body of knowledge of a spiritual tradition? Certainly the theologian is not necessarily the person of great faith. And perhaps it is not necessary to know any more than I already do to nourish this lifetime practice as a Buddhist. A wise person once said it is better to climb one mountain a hundred times, than to climb a hundred mountains.

Today is a lazy day and it has gone on an up and down path. After dinner last night I was talking to several nuns, including one visiting from Vermont. They were arguing against taking notes during the Dharma talks and I was trying to explain that I understood that point but there was also value in trying to save some impressions to share at home; sharing is so important to a marriage, family, friends, etc. In the end I wished I hadn't persisted in the argument. It went nowhere, and there are so few chances to interact, it seems I wasted one. What a silly discussion! And then this morning one of the young American nuns asked if she could borrow my journal for the February 6th Dharma notes. Go figure!

This morning I watched a Dharma talk by Thay from a retreat for businessmen. It was the first talk of the retreat so it was all about living in the present moment, breathing, walking meditation, etc. I just let the Dharma rain fall in the perfect comfort of familiarity. Then I went to the bookstore and got a phone card and some cash, in case I needed them. I also selected more postcards to write, some thank you notes, and some photos of Thay for gifts. There is little here in the shops for gift giving, except books and tapes. It is rather nice that Thay hasn't become an industry. For the Sangha, it must be a temptation to capitalize on his popularity.

After lunch I do my pot scrubbing duty (today's job for my family) and then fall asleep. We have a Beginning Anew ceremony — just the flower watering part where participants take turns being supportive to each other. I say just a few words about how great a roommate Miyo is, and thank Sister for bringing me a reminder of home by coming from Vermont. I get teary, which in all my life I have never understood. At times, strange times, the tears are so flowing, just welling and falling. As far back as I can remember tears have come this way to me.

"Confusion is better than being sure." (TNH) I'm doing very well!

We have dinner and afterwards the rest of my work family is at a meeting, so I have pots coming out of my ears. Then a nun opens the kitchen door where I am working. I'll be lucky not to catch pneumonia. The rain still has not stopped – day after day. You can see all the flowers coming up now, little bits of color nudging through the wet brown earth. It will be a spectacular springtime here in a short time.

I am getting quite comfortable in Plum Village now. I am like an old timer, explaining things to the newcomers. It is comfortable to know where things are, and what the routines and expectations are. At least for me it is significant. At times, I experience great peace. Marie said I have a happy personality, and although I don't think of myself that way, there certainly is happiness here. At times, I feel infused with deep joy. This, I know, is a result of the practice.

This morning Marie comes forward alone to receive the Fourteen Mindfulness Trainings. The format of the ceremony is similar to that of the Five Mindfulness Trainings. The Trainings are both provoking and magnificent to reflect upon.

The Fourteen Mindfulness Trainings

1. *The First Mindfulness Training: Openness*
   Aware of the suffering created by fanaticism and intolerance, we are determined not to be idolatrous about or bound to any doctrine, theory, or ideology, even Buddhist ones. Buddhist teachings are guiding means to help us learn to look deeply and to develop our understanding and compassion. They are not doctrines to fight, kill, or die for.

2. *The Second Mindfulness Training: Nonattachment to Views*
   Aware of the suffering created by attachment to views and wrong perceptions, we are determined to avoid being narrow-minded and bound to present views. We shall learn and practice nonattachment from views in order to be open to others' insights and experiences. We are aware that the knowledge we presently possess is not changeless, absolute truth. Truth is found in life, and we will observe life within

and around us in every moment, ready to learn throughout our lives.

3. *The Third Mindfulness Training: Freedom of Thought*
Aware of the suffering brought about when we impose our views on others, we are committed not to force others, even our children, by any means whatsoever – such as authority, threat, money, propaganda, or indoctrination – to adopt our views. We will respect the right of others to be different and to choose what to believe and how to decide. We will, however, help others renounce fanaticism and narrowness through compassionate dialogue.

4. *The Fourth Mindfulness Training: Awareness of Suffering*
Aware that looking deeply at the nature of suffering can help us develop compassion and find ways out of suffering, we are determined not to avoid or close our eyes before suffering. We are committed to finding ways, including personal contact, images, and sounds, to be with those who suffer, so we can understand their situation deeply and help them transform their suffering into compassion, peace and joy.

5. *The Fifth Mindfulness Training: Simple, Healthy Living*

Aware that true happiness is rooted in peace, solidity, freedom, compassion, and not in wealth or fame, we are determined not to take as the aim of our life fame, profit, wealth, or sensual pleasure, nor to accumulate wealth while millions are hungry and dying. We are committed to living simply and sharing our time, energy, and material resources with those in need. We will practice mindful consuming, not using alcohol, drugs, or any other products that bring toxins into our own and the collective body and consciousness.

6. *The Sixth Mindfulness Training: Dealing with Anger*

Aware that anger blocks communication and creates suffering, we are determined to take care of the energy of anger when it arises and to recognize and transform the seeds of anger that lie deep in our consciousness. When anger comes up, we are determined not to do or say anything, but to practice mindful breathing or mindful walking and acknowledge, embrace, and look deeply into our anger. We will learn to look with the eyes of compassion at those we think are the cause of our anger.

7. *The Seventh Mindfulness Training: Dwelling Happily in the Present Moment*
Aware that life is available only in the present moment and that it is possible to live happily in the here and now, we are committed to training ourselves to live deeply each moment of daily life. We will try not to lose ourselves in dispersion or be carried away by regrets about the past, worries about the future, or craving, anger, or jealousy in the present. We will practice mindful breathing to come back to what is happening in the present moment. We are determined to learn the art of mindful living by touching the wondrous, refreshing, and healing elements that are inside and around us, and by nourishing seeds of joy, peace, love, and understanding in ourselves, thus facilitating the work of transformation and healing in our consciousness.

8. *The Eight Mindfulness Training: Community and Communication*
Aware that lack of communication always brings separation and suffering, we are committed to training ourselves in the practice of compassionate listening and loving speech. We will learn to listen deeply without judging or reacting and refrain from uttering words that can create discord or cause the community to break. We will make every effort to keep communications

open and to reconcile and resolve all conflicts, however small.

9. *The Ninth Mindfulness Training: Truthful and Loving Speech*
Aware that words can create suffering or happiness, we are committed to learning to speak truthfully and constructively, using only words that inspire hope and confidence. We are determined not to say untruthful things for the sake of personal interest or to impress people, nor to utter words that might cause division or hatred. We will not spread news that we do not know to be certain nor criticize or condemn things of which we are not sure. We will do our best to speak out about situations of injustice, even when doing so may threaten our safety.

10. *The Tenth Mindfulness Training: Protecting the Sangha*
Aware that the essence and aim of a Sangha is the practice of understanding and compassion, we are determined not to use the Buddhist community for personal gain or profit or transform our community into a political instrument. A spiritual community should, however, take a clear stand against oppression and injustice and should strive to change the situation without engaging in partisan conflicts.

11. The Eleventh Mindfulness Training:
Right Livelihood
Aware that great violence and injustice have
been done to our environment and society,
we are committed not to live with a vocation
that is harmful to humans and nature. We
will do our best to select a livelihood that
helps realize our ideal of understanding
and compassion. Aware of global economic,
political and social realities, we will behave
responsibly as consumers and as citizens,
not investing in companies that deprive
others of their chance to live.

12. The Twelfth Mindfulness Training:
Reverence for Life
Aware that much suffering is caused by war
and conflict, we are determined to cultivate
nonviolence, understanding, and
compassion in our daily lives, to promote
peace education, mindful mediation, and
reconciliation within families, communities,
nations, and in the world. We are
determined not to kill and not to let others
kill. We will diligently practice deep looking
with our Sangha to discover better ways to
protect life and prevent war.

13. The Thirteenth Mindfulness Training:
Generosity
Aware of the suffering caused by
exploitation, social injustice, stealing, and
oppression, we are committed to cultivating

loving kindness and learning ways to work for the well-being of people, animals, plants, and minerals. We will practice generosity by sharing our time, energy, and material resources with those who are in need. We are determined not to steal and not to possess anything that should belong to others. We will respect the property of others, but will try to prevent others from profiting from human suffering or the suffering of other beings.

14. The Fourteenth Mindfulness Training: Right Conduct

(For lay members) Aware that sexual relations motivated by craving cannot dissipate the feeling of loneliness but will create more suffering, frustration, and isolation, we are determined not to engage in sexual relations without mutual understanding, love, and a long-term commitment. In sexual relations, we must be aware of future suffering that may be caused. We know that to preserve the happiness of ourselves and others, we must respect the rights and commitments of ourselves and others. We will do everything in our power to protect children from sexual abuse and to protect couples and families from being broken by sexual misconduct. We will treat our bodies with respect and preserve our vital energies (sexual, breath, spirit) for the realization of our bodhisattva ideal. We will be fully aware of the responsibility of bringing new lives into the world, and will meditate on the world into which we are bringing new beings.

Perhaps because we feel celebratory of Marie and her new commitment, lunch is especially good today: lentil soup with carrots, potatoes and greens, fennel baked with brie cheese and thin sliced nuts, zucchini and potatoes plain, and cabbage by Iris. I don't think there is a food processor here but Iris explains that you put the cabbage in one and process until it is very fine then just add half a cup of oil, half a cup of vinegar and salt and pepper. Everyone loves it. Maybe because it is so green and fresh – spring in a bowl!

We had a Five Mindfulness Training discussion this morning and Dharma discussion this afternoon. As brother Chris would say – I'm grouped out. There is a new schedule the community is trying out. We have meditation at five o'clock now and then supper with some free time after. Noble Silence is at nine. I actually like it much better. It is easier to sit before you eat, and when supper is over you don't have to wait and then go out again. All is done. I did have mopping to do here in Persimmon tonight, but it is eight o'clock and I'm all set for the evening.

The concept of interbeing, that all is connected, is powerful to me. It makes me pause and look at everything more carefully, mindfully. What I feel is missing for me here is the concept of the individual soul. It may be just ego but I find I'm quite attached to that idea. Ah, attachment again! But what is most important in Buddhism to me is not the intellectual theorizing – which Buddha warned us against getting caught in – but the practice. It is the source of liberation.

It is difficult to feel at home in my Catholic Church but the truth is, it is my home. I cannot envision that it will ever be a comfortable one for me. Several issues make me seek spiritual shelter elsewhere. First, I am a woman and I love my gender identity. I am deeply ashamed of the Church's treatment of my sex. Second, the world's population growth is a global crisis that in many quarters cannot even be discussed because of this Church. Certainly life is precious and needs protection, but the Church seems to see this in a very simplistic, narrow sense. Third, although I see a role for public positions and witness, beyond that, what right does the Church have to conduct other peoples' lives – those of different religions and cultures? There is such institutional arrogance and ethnocentrism. The "one, true Church" is a belief I cannot accept. And finally fourth, the curtailment of intellectual and spiritual inquiry by the hierarchy is totally offensive to me. This is a long-standing practice in the Church and how much has been lost because of it? This loss is not just for individuals, but for the possibility for a much more evolved institution, in step with the times and, at the same time, in step with the spirit of Jesus' teachings.

Wednesday, February 16

This morning Miyo receives the Five Mindfulness Trainings. I am so happy for her, knowing the support, guidance and peace they offer her for a lifetime.

My work duty this morning is to clean the barn! We are assigned regular chores but then we get these "special" assignments for working meditation. The barn is right next door to my residence hall and I have always looked at it with a fond imagining of days gone by filled with goats, horses, cows, and farm folk. Now, my perception changes. It is a dreary, dirty place full of stuff! Piles and piles of stuff! So it begins — sorting plant pots and taking their contents down to the garden, moving heavy, cumbersome stacks of plastic sheeting and disposing of others in the garbage, breaking down boxes, sorting, recycling, sweeping, etc. Every time I ask the nun if that is all, she gives me something else to do; sweep the veranda, wash the kitchen entrance, etc.

Sister Tamdin invites me to sit with her so I can have a hot cup of tea for a break. Yes, it is still raining. I remark to Sr.Tamdin that she has looked sad to me during the last week, and she explains that it is because her position in the community is unclear. She waits to hear if they will accept her. She feels like she is in a haze. We discuss Asian circular thinking, as opposed to the Western linear thinking, for a bit. Such a nice woman! A sister comes over and we are told not to talk during working meditation time (but it is common, including the nuns!). I decide to skip walking meditation and take a hot shower and wash some clothes.

This afternoon I take some Advil and rest after lunch. Seems like farm life is not for me! Then we go to the big zendo for a videotaped Dharma talk since Sr. Jina is not available for the question and answer session. Thay starts by talking about anger but it is really a talk on love, so beautiful and evocative. Then we have afternoon sitting in the big zendo. I am very distracted. Broadway show tunes keep coming, cheery, but really! I am not Whoopie Goldberg in "Sister Act!" I think I'm just ready to leave and be with my family. Had the usual after dinner routine of putting away pots and mopping. Now it's eight o'clock and the day is done.

Thursday, February 17

Still raining! I feel like I will never be clean, warm and dry again! This morning we leave for Thay's Dharma talk in New Hamlet at 6:30. Since I was too lazy to carry a flashlight, it is pitch black everywhere. My assignment on the community board is the Golf car. Never heard of one! So I wander the parking lot quietly asking rushing dark forms, "Do you know which car is the Golf?" And no one does until Sr. Jina comes along. Not only does she know, but she takes me right there. My guardian angel!

The Dharma talk continues the Sutra study and then last week's talk on consciousness. I keep wanting to drift off for some reason. It's the first time I have been sleepy during a Dharma talk here. Maybe because there was no breakfast and yesterday there was so much physical activity. Also, last night's dinner was soup, pasta and potatoes, not as well balanced as usual. Whatever the reason for such torpor, I manage to struggle with it and stay awake.

Formal lunch is in the big zendo and Thay has three monks sing – one in Spanish, one in French and then the younger monk from the Tibetan tradition. Looking helplessly around the hall, he calls on his fellows in residence, one additional monk and two sisters. They are not prepared for this command performance. Tibetans do not sing they claim, but chant. So awkwardly they give a chant a good, spirited, self-conscious try while everyone cheers them on.

After lunch we have places we could go for an hour or two of rest, separated by gender, and lay and monastic. I go to the little zendo which is all women, but both lay and monastic. People get confused about all the designations and directions but no one minds that I could tell. Anyway, the weather is so miserable people are trying to rest near the heaters but they don't seem to be turned on.

Tea meditation for the monastics was separate as they said goodbye to the Suba, the visiting senior nuns from Vietnam. The lay residents had a large tea meditation. There seemed to be more of us today. We all sat in a large circle, drank our tea and ate our cake in silence after the bell. Then we went half way around introducing ourselves, had a song, and finished introductions. There were a number of songs for over two and a half hours – French, Spanish, English, Hindi, South African, Vietnamese, German, and more. It was impressive in scope but, for me, too long.

When we signed up for the day we could choose to come back before dinner or after. So Miyo and I signed up for the early return in a car with the Tibetan nuns. A young sister quietly drove us. When we got back to Lower Hamlet, the Tibetan nuns asked about supper and Sister told us if we did not stay for the supper the New Hamlet sisters had prepared, there was none! Miyo and I got tea in the dining hall and Miyo took her cup back to wash, and see if she could get something to eat. The same nun was in the kitchen eating. Don't know what her problem is! Later, after we settled in our room, Miyo went to the kitchen again and brought back a small feast of cellophane noodles with cauliflower and potato salad. Novices had been out jogging and were in the kitchen cooking. Others had joined in, so Miyo was supported. We set up our treasured picnic on our floor and stayed up talking as we did the night before, mostly about her boyfriend from Africa, moving there, and her family's reaction to both. She is delightful company and I will miss her!

Now I am curled up on my bed mulling over the Dharma talk. The New Hamlet's large zendo, Full Moon Meditation Hall, gave a teaching itself. It has an area of the wall with portraits of spiritual ancestors – including Jesus. Now if only we could find a place for Buddha in our churches!

Here are some sprinkles of today's Dharma rain from Thay:
If you look in the ultimate dimension you are already a Buddha. You don't have to do anything. You only have to laugh, enjoy! In the ultimate dimension, the sea pirate has Buddha nature. In the historic dimension he is a bad man. When we see dependent co-arising we accept things as they are and live in joy.

We have an upside down perception believing in a separate self and permanence. This creates a world of delusion and makes us suffer.

If we love someone we construct an image that is not that person. We focus on one wrong thing and forget the 99 good. We marry, and are shocked! We make many, many wrong images. We bring hurt and fear from childhood wounds.

Thay taught on looking deeply as he gazed at the orchids in front of him and asked if they are a mental construction or reality. He noted that we are lucky to have the chance to look deeply. The degree of mindfulness depends on each person. If there are 100 people, there are 100 perceptions. All wrong. We are closer to reality when we see all is impermanent, when we see interdependence and many conditions. In the negative seeds of suffering, there is enlightenment. Look deeply and anger is transformed into the mind of love. Thay asked how we could have a vision that transcends the duality of matter and consciousness as separate. He gave examples of particle and wave merging into wavicle. He posed the question – dead or alive? In reality all the time we are both. We are also not just male or female. When we transcend dualism we are peaceful, happy, liberated.

A nun brought a candle up to the platform and Thay spoke. Consciousness is like the flame of a candle; its nature is impermanence. The supporting conditions for the flame are the sister holding the candle, the candle, the match, air, etc. When it is manifested, you believe it exists. Before, you say it does not exist. But the flame is free from this duality. The presence of the flame is in the non-flame elements. The nature of the flame is that it is dying every moment, neither the same nor different. There are multi-flames succeeding each other. The elements are changing. The former second's flame is the cause of the present flame, is the cause of the next flame, etc. It can only be for a fraction of a second. Flame is free from birth and death and the nature of consciousness is impermanence.

Thay said we are always looking for permanence so we are easily caught. We want heaven, Nirvana, the Buddha, to be permanent entities. It is a childish kind of hope, a longing to go back to the womb. When we see consciousness correctly as momentary, ever changing, we see interbeing. Only understanding from deep looking will free you from opposites and give the greatest gift of all — nonfear.

Friday, February 18

This morning I missed sitting – woke in the middle of the night and couldn't sleep again so I just rested. Miyo said few people were there; even the nuns were missing.

After breakfast my name was on the board for working meditation – clean the cars! I got out of it because I was cooking lunch beginning at 9:30. Boy, am I glad to be cooking. Cleaning cars wouldn't normally be bad but, guess what – it's still raining! Incense is lit in the kitchen before we begin and Elena is keeping Noble Silence so we all do, to support her. Cooking is pleasant, mindful, peaceful. This tranquility is broken at eleven. There is walking meditation so Elena wants one of us two helpers to go. I don't want to go but Corrine, who must be about eighteen years old, pleads that the reason she is wearing a hat is because she is having trouble with her ears. So Elena sends me to walk for us all, out in the deluge. It is miserable, but mindfully miserable.

After lunch I come back and crawl under the covers to listen to music since I just can't get warm. I sleep a little then get up to sort through papers and odds and ends, pre-packing.

Sorry to say good-bye to Miyo. She will be one of my favorites from here. Before she leaves we go to the pay phones and confirm my own flights. I hate to think where my French would have taken me.

Tomorrow will be my last full day here. Already bittersweet feelings of leave-taking are occurring. Sunday I'm off early to Spain to reunite with Shanti, Chandan and Tom. I'm ready to make the transition.

This morning it is pouring during the first half of sitting. We do our slow walking and as I approach my cushion I catch sight of Thay out of the corner of my eye. I can't believe it, but there he is, just a few cushions away in the row in front of me. We all face the center and he begins a chant practice. The lights are on now so we can all see each other clearly. Thay gives instructions to the nun who is bell master. He explains that this person is the leader of the chant, striking the bell not at the end but near, so all would know when to stop. The young Vietnamese nun takes his instructions on particular parts calmly, without any expression. Thay has the drum. He tells us about chanting by heart in Sanskrit, and how beautiful the sound of 100 monks chanting in the evening is; about how a chant of the Heart Sutra, is like a flock of birds going along on one note with just some dips.

Then Thay invites us all to form a circle around him. This is the dream experience of Plum Village for me. There are only about twenty-five of us and Thay speaks softly to us like we are just in conversation. Some of the points he makes are: the practice is about relationships; it is not just about form. We sit at formal lunch to eat not just food, but the energy of the Sangha. We sit as a Sangha. It is important for there to be joy in the community. He asks several nuns by name how they are. (Everyone is fine when he asks, it seems!) He asks about the aspiring novices and the three from Lower Hamlet raise their hands. He reports that there are two more at New Hamlet and a young man who wants to be a monk at Upper Hamlet. He talks about how everyone has talents, and how they should make their wishes about what they want known to their Abbess. Then they can practice whatever it is and become good at it, even if they are not good at it in the beginning. He tells them to write to the Abbess. Thay then asks why there are no suggestions in the suggestion box. He is always thinking of suggestions. (This is said very caringly, encouraging them to come forth.) He reports that in the Upper Hamlet one of the monks wants a tennis court, and he wants a piano for the New Hamlet because it causes joy. He also says one of the meditation halls needs additional roofing because water is getting in, but no surprise there! Water is everywhere!

Thay reflects that the last two Dharma talks summed up the important message of the winter retreat. He refers to the various viewpoints on consciousness and matter and notes how scientists need spirituality, especially in this 21st century. Otherwise it will be a dangerous time.

Thay has breakfast in the dining room. They close all the doors except the one through the kitchen, as they did the other time he had breakfast with us. This is so there is no draft on him. Today I did not get to do his dishes! Last time I did, not realizing they were his. They were green, rectangular ceramic plates with a bamboo design. Not expensive, but simple and pleasing. As far as I can see, he is spoiled only in these small ways, reflections of the loving attention that surrounds him.

My work assignment today is to clean the Red Candle Zendo where we had just been together with Thay. Alone I note the symmetry of this last assignment, since it was also my first. With special love and care, I prepare the zendo wondering if I'll ever come here again. Then I come back to the present moment and find peace, always a practice.

After lunch a beautiful French nun calls my taxi for tomorrow morning, so here's hoping! She takes me aside to say she is sorry not to have had the opportunity to get to know me. She explains that it used to be different, with more interaction between monastics and lay visitors, which she felt was good for the monastics, as well as the visitors. Perhaps it will be that way again. This is still a young community and after all, all is change! The sun is out! Happy day!

At five o'clock meditation Sister Jina introduces the Invitation Ceremony that will be taking place this evening. In the Buddha's time the monks spent most of their time traveling, teaching the Dharma. During the winter, or rainy season, they came together for several months because travel was difficult and dangerous. It was their opportunity to practice together. Since these early days, the winter retreat has been a tradition of Buddhist communities. In this tradition, the number of winter retreats they have participated in determines the age of seniority of a monk or nun. So in this case, Sister Jina says, it is good to advance in years. There is a related ceremony at the beginning of the retreat. Tonight those here for all three months, lay and monastic, will invite a sister to shine light on their practice. In past years this took several hours, so now the evaluation, or "encouraging words", is already written out. The ceremony will start with the youngest and then work its way up. When all the lay people are done, they have to leave and the monastics do their own light shining.

During the afternoon I am sorting, packing and putting out tomorrow's clothes, luxuriously using three of the four beds, when one of the nuns knocks. I have a new roommate! Boy, am I surprised! The difficulty, especially for her, is that she doesn't speak any English. I explain to Sister that I don't speak French and I am leaving early tomorrow morning, not going to Upper Hamlet. She tells mc to show the new arrival around here and quickly goes off. This poor woman, Magdeline, has never been here before! I go and find Corrine and she takes her under her more comfortable, French wing.

All went smoothly this morning. I left as I came, alone in the Hamlet taking photographs in the quiet morning light. At last it is a beautiful day. I'm so glad for all the Plum Villagers to have this day to end winter retreat on – and for me to fly on.

It will be a while before I fully understand this time and know its fruits. The challenge was real and not exactly what was expected. But my time became more relaxed and fulfilling as the days passed and the Buddha, the Dharma, and the Sangha blessed me.

There has been a sort of shifting in me, a defining. Most critical to me right now are mindfulness and the insight it brings. The strength and great beauty of the Buddha's and Thay's teachings are my path to mindfulness. But the Christian experience of my formative years determines who I am to a great extent, and I treasure that history. Like all in this world, I am constant change.

So I leave with a warm heart for these gentle, radiant people and their work. I am full of gratitude that Thay exists in our miraculous, but wounded, world. How lucky I have been to have these weeks, and the support of my loved ones to make them happen. But if I never return to Plum Village, that is fine. The really important gift, the

Dharma, is found anywhere, anytime, in the teachings of the Buddha brought to us by Thay. The Sangha is universal.

"There is no way to happiness.
Happiness is the way."

EPILOGUE

As I prepare to put this little book to bed, I cannot help but reflect on how much has changed in the short time since these events took place. The trip that is portrayed here took place as the millennium turned. At Plum Village, our celebration of the coming age was marked by festivities both traditionally Vietnamese and international in flavor. This alone made it a celebration of hope, and Thay's presence made it a joy.

The mood today is significantly different. The first anniversary of the World Trade Center attacks of September 11, 2001 has come and gone and we are still stabilizing from those horrible shockwaves. My home is just two and a half hours north of Ground Zero. All of us here seem to know people who died, were injured, displaced, widowed, orphaned, or affected in some way. We are in the turbulent, long wake of the tragedy. But indeed the whole country, and much of the world, is identifying with New York. And now, for a Buddhist, this is where the rubber meets the road.

How can one claim not to want to fight such terror? How can one not want revenge? Justice? How can one not want to rid the world of such menacing threats to more innocents? Thay has spoken and written eloquently on the need to stop all violence, on the need to understand the minds of those who have committed these crimes of terrorism, on the need to seek the root causes of violence. I have read it all. And I have sat and meditated. It has helped, with answers, and with calm.

I also have found refuge in the Buddha, the Dharma and the Sangha and now I fully understand why taking those refuges is so central to the practice. The very word "refuge" now resonates with me. We take comfort in the Buddha and his teachings and in those who are learning to live according to them with us. I am blessed to belong to a small group of aspirants to the Order of Interbeing, and I sit with my local Sangha. It is this support that allows us to be comforted when we feel out of step with others. And it allows us to bring a peaceful and loving presence to all at a time when there are high emotions, fear and misunderstanding.

Do I have answers? No, but I have increasing numbers of questions, and that is a step forward. Quick answers are bound to be incomplete and wrong. I know that I am grateful not to be in a position of making governmental policy in these difficult times; I pray for those who are. I know that I would not want to kill, and I wish I could say here that I would not kill, but I understand I am capable of killing. I understand my countrymen and women who are now walking through treacherous lands with rifles on their backs, seeking resolution to our national pain. And I understand the fanatical mindset of the Islamic men and women who think they are the only redeemed. My practice is to do the loving-kindness meditation for them all. At times it is hard. I have taught refugees from Afghanistan for over a dozen years and I have witnessed their suffering in mind, body and spirit. 9-11-01 did not surprise me. It only surprised me it took so long to get here. What do we do about the ones who have their evil seeds so well watered? How do we protect others, and our way of life under the Constitution? What changes need to be made here and abroad? How can all peoples make this a more tolerant world? Is peace possible? My mind spins with it all, but I take it back to the cushion and I am able to enter the present moment. Ah, there is peace.

Glossary

An Interpretation of Terms by the Author

ABBESS – The leader of the community of nuns.

ABBOT — The leader of the community of monks.

BODHISATTVA – A being on the path to enlightenment who strives to help others.

BUDDHA – This title means one who is awake. The historical figure, Siddhartha Gautama (566-486BC), who taught the path to enlightenment, is commonly known as the Buddha.

BUDDHA NATURE – The potential for good within each person that is always available.

CENTERING – Letting go of all distractions and entering the present.

CENTERING PRAYER – A Christian practice of prayer that is contemplative and meditative. It focuses on opening and listening to God.

DHARMA – The Buddhist teachings.

DHARMA TEACHER – A lay person, or monastic, who is recognized as a teacher of the Dharma and formally receives this responsibility and honor through a lamp transmission ceremony.

THE EIGHT FOLD PATH – The eight practices that relieve suffering: right view, right thought, right speech, right action, right livelihood, right effort, right awareness, and right concentration.

ENLIGHTENMENT – The ultimate state of liberation from all suffering.

THE FOUR NOBLE TRUTHS – 1. Suffering exists. 2. There are causes of suffering. 3. It is possible to cease the causes of suffering. 4. There is a path to remove the causes of suffering.

MEDITATION – The quieting and training of the mind that leads to transformation.

MINDFULNESS – Living in the present moment with awareness.

MINDFULNESS TRAININGS – Thich Nhat Hanh's modern statement of the Five Precepts.

ORDER OF INTERBEING – The Order established by Thich Nhat Hanh that takes and practices the vows of the Fourteen Mindfulness Trainings.

SANGHA – The community of Buddhist practitioners.

SUTRA – The teachings of the Buddha in written or oral form.

TET – The New Year celebration of the Vietnamese people.

THE THREE JEWELS – The Buddha, the Dharma and the Sangha.

THE TRIPLE JEMS – The Buddha, the Dharma and the Sangha.

WALKING MEDITATION – A form of meditation that centers on the breath but includes the act of walking, usually in a slow manner.

YOGA – The ancient Indian spiritual practice that includes asanas, or physical postures, pranayam, or breath work, and meditation.

ZABUTON – The rectangular cushion that the zafu sits on.

ZAFU – The round cushion used for meditation.

ZENDO – The meditation hall.

Order Form

Please send _Visiting Thich Nhah Hanh: An American in Plum Village_ to:

Name_____

Street_____

City_____State_____Zip_____

_____**Number of copies at $8.95 each**   _____

Shipping   _____
(In Canada and the U.S., $2.00 for the first book, and $.50 for each additional book. International orders $4.00 for fewer than 5 books.)
Sales Tax
(New York State residents add tax at local rate)   _____

Total   _____

Gift Recipient

Name_____

Street_____

City_____State_____Zip_____

Please include your phone number in case there are any questions concerning your order. (   ) _____—_____

Enclose check or money order to:

Anathapindika Press
PO Box 9262
Schenectady, NY 12309